W9-CLJ-621

BLACK HOLE, GREEN CARD

The Disappearance of Ireland

Patricia Ferreira
June 20, 1994
Dublin, Ireland

By the same author

From Raven Arts Press

The Southern Question
No More Heroes
A Mass for Jesse James

From New Island Books

Tom Murphy: The Politics of Magic

BLACK HOLE,

The disappearance of Ireland

GREEN CARD

FINTAN O'TOOLE

Dublin

BLACK HOLE, GREEN CARD
The Disappearance of Ireland
is first published in 1994 by
New Island Books,
2, Brookside,
Dundrum Road,
Dublin 14.

Copyright © Fintan O'Toole, 1994

ISBN 1 874597 01 4

New Island Books receives financial assistance
from
The Arts Council (An Chomhairle Ealaíon),
Dublin, Ireland.

Cover design by Jon Berkeley.
Typeset by Graphic Resources.
Printed in Ireland by Colour Books Ltd.

Contents

for
Colm Tóibín

INTRODUCTION

My parents' wedding photographs always remind me of a frontier town in an old Western. To prize open the mock mother-of-pearl covers of the wedding album is to enter a world of strange contrasts. There they are, elegant and radiant, wrapped in the proud formality of the 1950s, the elaborate dress and veil, the clean lines of my father's bespoke suit. They are emblems of a great continuity, of a seriousness and respectability forged over generations of struggle against squalor and dirt, against poverty and fecklessness. Their adamant dignity sparkles like a diamond hard-won from the dust and muck.

What gives the pictures their air of High Noon though, of a respectable wedding threatened by the dangers of a frontier town, is the setting. The church, which should be dark with gothic curves or bright with baroque tracery is merely dull with the blank stare of unadorned concrete. It is not really a church at all, but a temporary building slapped up to serve a hastily-conceived new suburb while the real one is still being built. It has no elegance and no resonance. It may have been consecrated by the wave of a bishop's hand, but it is unconsecrated by those holier things, by the skill of craftsmen or by the hopes and dreams of generations. Yet, for me, because of those photographs, it has to serve as one of those images of tradition and remembrance that we all carry around in our heads.

That ramshackle place, raw and temporary and forever unfinished, has to serve as the locus of an ordered and secure past. Strangely, though it still looks temporary after 40 years, it is still there, still an ugly shell of windowless breeze-block with a reinforced steel door at one side. And while the huge, windy church that replaced it now looks dated, ineffably of its time, the very blankness and ugliness of the temporary structure make it curiously timeless. Built without design or intention, it is not marked by the designs or intentions of any one decade. It could be the newest public building on the estate instead of the oldest. While families and lives come and go around it, it abides, a monument to the permanently temporary nature of the new Ireland whose frontier it once occupied.

With time, indeed, the building took on its own eerie importance. There was something strange about having this deconsecrated church down the road from the real one. It had the mysterious, ghostly presence of a wrecked ship at the mouth of a busy harbour, or a deserted village chanced upon in the quiet hills. And, indeed, it became a kind of alternative church, a site for a different sort of communion entered into by the disaffected young, the holy bread of sex and the heady wine of rock and roll. When I was about ten, the modern world, in all its shocking glory, arrived at this now-secularised church.

What happened was ordinary enough in its beginnings but deeply shocking in its repercussions. It began as a set of actions from the 1950s and ended as one from the 1980s. On a Wednesday evening in 1968, at the youth club hop in that still-temporary building where my parents were married, a priest arrived to find the lights down low and the couples clinched in too-sinful embrace. The dance was broken up, the dancers sent home. It was a small and clichéd drama, a tired reprise of a scene played out in parish halls and at crossroads all over de Valera's Ireland. It was the shocking response to it that marked the death of that Ireland.

Instead of burning with shame as the scandal was whispered around the parish, the dancers muttered together and let their anger fester. At ten o'clock Mass the next Sunday, they acted. They arrived early and en masse, and sat in the front two rows, facing the pulpit. As the parish priest rose for his sermon, they stood up and walked out, down the centre aisle, past gaping mothers and spluttering fathers, stilling the fingers that told the beads and silencing the lips that mouthed the pious murmurs. They would come back a few weeks later, defeated and cowed, never realising that they had dragged a whole world behind them in their footsteps when they walked out that door. They lost the battle but won a war they hardly knew they were fighting.

It is said that Haile Selaisse's reign as Emperor of Ethiopia ended, not when he was eventually overthrown by the army, but when, a few years earlier, a disaffected young official whom he was removing from his post, turned and walked out of the palace, not backwards and bowing, as custom demanded, but with his back to the Emperor and his head held high. From that moment the empire was doomed. In the same way, and with the same inevitability, an empire of certainties was doomed in our parish that day. An authority had been lost and could never be regained.

In 1992, fifteen years after I had moved out of the parish, my eye was drawn to a newspaper headline. "Priest shocked over rave drugs party held in parish bingo hall," it said. "A Dublin priest," went the first paragraph, "who hired out his parish hall for a 'fiftieth wedding anniversary' at the weekend was shocked to discover it was used for a rave acid house party instead, which was raided by gardai." The hall, of course, was that same temporary building in which my parents were married and from which the beginning of the disappearance of an old Ireland took, for us, its local habitation and its name.

The incident was a wilder, more dramatic but somehow less significant replay of those events of twenty-five years ago. The noise had woken people in the surrounding houses in the small hours of Sunday morning. The guards had been called. At 2 a.m. the ravers locked the doors with 200 people inside and the ecstacy-driven dancing continued for three hours.

Finally, after dawn, the police and the parish priest stormed the hall. The priest took to the stage under the flashing lights and screamed at the dancers to stop. No one minded his distress very much. The police dismantled the sound equipment and the lighting rig and took it all away. The dancers yawned and went out into the early light that was washing the playing fields a new bright green and glinting off the aluminium window frames that have long since replaced the Corporation's handiwork. It was Sunday morning and time for bed.

The incident was good for a natter after Mass, a juicier morsel of gossip than your man's indiscretions in the pub, or your woman's operation for cancer. But there was no profound shock. A priest asked to comment shrugged and said, "These raves are happening all over the place now, it's very hard to stop them." And anyway, the whole thing, organised and confident as it was, seemed rather benign compared to the lonely, desperate deaths from heroin that scarred this parish a few years back. A mould, once broken, cannot be broken again, and this one had split with a quieter but much more disquieting crack twenty-five years ago.

The ravers, of course, wouldn't be awake for Mass, even if they wanted to go. While the faithful gathered, they would be drifting into psychadelic dreams, not to be woken till the rich smell of the Sunday roast had penetrated upstairs to lure them from sleep. In the church, the front two rows would be safely filled with pious old ladies, not with protestors. The temporary hall had finally triumphed over the permanent church. The contingent, makeshift society was now more real than the illusions of permanence and tradition. The parish priest, not the young dancers in the hall, was now the lonely protestor, the bewildered voice crying out in the flashing light. It is hard to suppress a twinge of pathos, but better to move on, knowing, at least, where we are now.

The place my parents married into was still a known country. It was a place where everything was known about you, where, if you turned the lights down low, the doors would open and you were caught. The place we have become is a place where a High Court judge, Mr Justice

Lynch, having heard eight months of detailed evidence about a small tragedy in County Kerry could feel it necessary to write, in his judicial report, quoting James Thurber, that "we live man and worm, in an age where almost everything can mean almost anything."

In the time between my parents' wedding and the all-night rave, the capacity to know itself had gradually been lost to the country. The fixed points of the compass of life — church, nation, family — had been unsettled. In truth, the place my parents had come to was already a new kind of Ireland, one where tradition and place and history were but shallow-rooted transplants. The physical land-marks of the area — the quarry, the ashpits where my bare-footed uncle burned his feet, the old mills and fields — had been obliterated, and a new life of streets and houses laid over their ruins.

In three decades Ireland became a place where much more was known about individual lives, but where larger realities became literally unknown. In the 1990s, if you ask some basic questions, questions that in most countries would be merely preliminary, you get deeply uncertain answers. Because the economy is dominated by multinational companies, and because it is in their interests to exaggerate for taxation purposes the extent of their Irish profits, we do not know the GNP of the country or the scale of its exports.

Three quarters of Irish manufactured exports are from foreign-owned multinationals, which import most of their inputs and export most of their profits. The cost of components imported for assembly in Ireland is exaggerated, the extent of exports overstated and the profits invisibly exported through the Black Hole. Thus, as economists mildly express it, "data on their output give a rather misleading impression of their contribution to the economy." About 60 per cent of the value of these export sales leaves the country in the form either of payments for bought-in components or of repatriated profits. In the most real sense imaginable — wealth, jobs, the stuff of economic life — Ireland drains away, disappears, and leaves a reality that can only be guessed at.

Just as the wealth that disappears is unquantifiable, so are the people. The number of emigrants from Ireland in the last decade is unknown. The Cork based geographer Jim McLaughlin has summed up the state of knowledge in this area by saying that "not the least of the paradoxes surrounding its study is the fact that we probably know more about the emigration of farm labourers from post-Famine Ireland, and the status of Irish immigrants in late-Victorian England than we know about emigration among contemporary school leavers and young adults." Thus for instance, estimates of the number of illegal Irish immigrants in New York city alone vary between 40,000 and 100,000. They are by their nature invisible — undocumented, unregistered, often unable even to use their own names.

We know, for instance, that the population of the Republic fell by 0.4% in the 1991 census compared with the 1986 census, the first such fall since the transformations of the 1960s got underway. We also know that huge numbers of young people left the country in the late 1980s. But figures for net emigration tell only a part of the story. To take the number of emigrants and to subtract from it the number of immigrants gives you a crude picture of the process. That process itself, however, is almost certainly a vastly complex and shifting one, with the same people going and coming back in accordance with the state of the British, American and European economies.

The picture hidden by the statistics is a staggering one. The best estimates are that about 1 in every 12 people living in the Republic in 1982 (i.e 289,000 people) had emigrated by 1989, when the outflows were temporarily staunched by recessions in Britain and the United States. Some of these people went and stayed gone. Some came back, left again, came back again. Some of those who went were themsleves the children of emigrants who returned in the 1960s. Taken all in all, you get a profoundly unsettled society, one on which we have no real fix.

In a study by Jim McLaughlin in Cork city, South Limerick, South Kerry, East Galway, and North Donegal, a quarter of the families surveyed had at least one member living abroad. Almost one in three of the Donegal families had a member who had recently emigrated, and over one in ten of these families had four or more emigrants. "A large numbers of homes here," he says "could be classified as 'transnational households'."

And the actual emigrants are themselves only a subset of the much wider pool of people who see themselves as potential emigrants and understand their future as possibly taking place elsewhere. The 60 per cent of 16 to 24 year-olds who told an Irish Times/MRBI survey in 1987 that they had contemplated emigration and the 70 per cent who said that Ireland did not offer them a good future are cyphers of this larger, mental and spiritual emigration. Amongst the young, a large majority are, in the hopes and dreams and mental images of a future life, citizens of the Republic of Elsewhere.

Thus, as well as holding Irish passports, many thousands hold Donnelly and Morrison visas even though they continue to live in Ireland. The huge numbers of young people who put their names in for the Green Card lotteries, and the large but unknown number of winners who pretend to the American authorities that they are resident in the United States by entering the country once a year represent a strange reservoir of psychic emigrants, people who live in Ireland but whose mental horizons incorporate America as either an aspiration, a fail-safe, or both.

"A nation" says Leopold Bloom under pressure "is the same people living in the same place." And then, under more pressure, he adds "Or also living in different places." Ireland invented itself under the auspices of the first of those attempted definitions. The conjunction of "same people" and "same place", conveniently reinforced by partition, made a thing called "Ireland". Now, as we face the disappearance of Ireland under the pressures of economics, of geography, of the collapse of the religious monolith which was inseparable from our self-definition, we are left with no option but to add Bloom's contradictory corrective about different places. And even that may not be enough. We live in different places, but are we the "same people"? Only if we can understand sameness in a way that incorporates difference, that brooks contradictions and that is comfortable with the idea that the only fixed Irish identity and the only useful Irish tradition is the Irish tradition of not having a fixed identity.

The essays in this book are an attempt to explore some of the ways in which the disappearance of a knowable Ireland has manifested itself in Irish life in the 1990s. They deal with politics, history, landscape, religion and culture. But they do not pretend to deal with any of these areas comprehensively. Their aim is to be suggestive and exploratory rather than comprehensive or dogmatic. They are written, as Bloom's definition is given, under pressure of events, and in full awareness that at any moment it will be necessary to add "Or also..."

Place

THE LIE OF THE LAND

Some Thoughts on the Map of Ireland

1.

In January, 1994, An Post moved its sorting operations onto a new computerised system. Problems began when the computer starting reading the first place name on each address as the crucial one, so that letters for Dublin Road, Galway, went to Dublin and letters for Cork Street, Dublin went to Cork. On RTE radio, the company's chief executive admitted that a letter addressed to a house called Arizona somewhere in the Midlands went to Arizona. Who is to say that the computer was not right, that the confusion was not, in its own way, a kind of truth?

In May, 1993 the Committee of Public Accounts of Dail Eireann discovered that Ireland had disappeared. Or rather, that 85,000 Irelands had disappeared. James V. Rogers, accounting officer of the Ordnance Survey, told the committee that 85,000 maps of Ireland were mysteriously unaccounted for. A stocktaking in March, 1992 had shown up this discrepancy between the number of maps sold and the number actually in stock. The committee spent an hour pondering the question of what might have happened to so many representations of the country.

Sean Doherty, the former Fianna Fáil Minister for Justice, whose revelations about phone tapping had led to the downfall of Charles Haughey as Taoiseach in early 1992, took a particular interest in the question. Was it possible, he asked, that the maps might never have existed?

"Yes," said Mr Rogers, "that is possible."

"There is no loss of something that never existed," said Sean Doherty.

But if they had existed, wondered Senator Martin Cullen, how much space would they have taken up? After all, you could hardly hide that many Irelands in a corner somewhere. Maybe they had been spirited away?

Supposing the maps did occupy space, Sean Doherty insisted, how much space would it be?

"Do you mean linear footage?" asked Mr Rogers.

And so the metaphysicians pondered, looking for their lost country, until, in the end, Sean Doherty brought the discussion to a close with the warning that "We may have to search where we never searched before."

This comic mystery story, staged at the heart of political power in Ireland, was more than usually symbolic. These disappeared Irelands, these lost maps of the island, these questions of how much space something that does not exist might take up, expressed in their own way a real sense of a place that has slipped away. A map, after all, is a convenient fiction, a more or less confident representation of the shape a place might take if only you could see it. While the place itself persists, the map, the visual and ideological convention that allows us to call that place "Ireland" has been slipping away. Its co-ordinates, its longitudes and latitudes, refuse to hold their shape.

2.

In this Chart, I have laide down no land nor figur'd out any shore but what I saw myself, and thus far the Chart may be depended on.

— The Journals of Captain James Cook On His Voyages Of Discovery, 1768-1771.

16

On the original map of the eastern shores of Australia charted on Captain Cook's Endeavour voyage, a large undulating band of letters follows the course of the carefully plotted coast. The letters form the words NEW SOUTH WALES, DISC. 1770. They are written more or less vertically, from the bottom up, but they twist in a graceful double arc. They curve inwards from Bateman Bay to Point Danger, as the coast does, and then, like the coast, curve outward again towards Cape Cleveland, before tapering outwards again to Trinity Bay. When these words were written on the map, borrowing the name of a submerged country thousands of miles away, the place they gave that name to was largely unknown to those who wrote them. And indeed, with their shape that describes a voyage, they seem to refer not to a fixed place at all, but to a journey that has just been made. Looking at them, you realise that the map, as Paul Carter has pointed out, "was from the beginning, designed to record particular information. As the spaces on its grid were written over, there was revealed a palimpsest of the explorer's experience, a criss-cross of routes gradually thickening and congealing into fixed seas and lands. In this context, the rubric 'New South Wales, Disc. 1770' named not so much a country but, by the direction of its writing, the course of a journey."

This serpentine rubric on a map of exploration, naming the course of a journey but reminiscent of a remembered place called Wales, seems appropriate to Ireland in the 1990s. These literally twisted words, projecting the name of a historic place onto a blank and uncharted space, belong to what Carter calls "Cook's geo-graphy, his writing of lands," a similar geography to that in which the Irish are now engaged. If they lay out a country, it is, as Cook boasted, "no land but what I saw myself", a country whose map is no more nor less than the chart of personal experience and personal journeys. In a country like Ireland, whose modern history is shaped by the personal journeys of the emigrant, any accurate map of the land must be a map, not of an island, but of a shoreline seen from the water, a set of contours shaped, not by geography, but by voyages. The shape of the island is the shape of all the journeys around it that a history of emigration has set in motion.

As it happens, modern geometry has given a new sanction to this kind of subjective map-making. In his *Fractal Geometry of Nature*, the mathematician Benoit Mandlebrot asks the apparently simple question "how long is the coast of Britain?" The coast is obviously not smooth and regular. It goes in and out in bays and estuaries and promontories and capes. If you measure it at one hundred miles to an inch, all of these irregularities appear. But if you measure it at twenty miles to an inch, new bays open up on the coastlines of promontories and new promontories jut out from the sides of bays. When you measure these as well, the coastline gets longer. At a mile to an inch it is even longer... and so on, until you crawl around on your hands and knees measuring the bumps on the side of each rock that makes up the coast. The more accurately you measure it, the more uncertain it becomes. What matters, in the end, is your point of view. Mandlebrot compares the length of the border between Spain and Portugal in a Portugese and a Spanish atlas. In the former it is twenty per cent longer than in the latter, not because the territory is disputed, but because Spanish surveyors used a larger scale, and thus measured fewer squiggles.

So it is with the map of Ireland. The closer you look, the more accurately you take into account the actual experiences of the people born on the island, the more unstable the coastline becomes. Subjectively, using the small scale to measure the inlets and outflows of human life, the coastline expands to breaking point, scattering the inhabitants of the island half way around the globe.

Emigration means, quite simply, that the people and the land are no longer co-terminous. In this sense, the map of

Ireland is a lie. The lie of the land is that there is a place called "Ireland" inhabited by the Irish people, a place with a history, a culture, a society. Yet the central fact of that history is that, over 150 years, much of it has happened elsewhere, in Chicago and Coventry, in Boston and Birmingham, in Hell's Kitchen and Camden Town. The central fact of that culture is that it knows no borders. The central fact of that society is that it is porous and diffuse, that its apparent stability is maintained only at the cost of the continual export of its instabilities.

It was an Irishman, Oscar Wilde, who wrote that "a map of the world that does not include Utopia is not worth even glancing at, for it leaves out the one country at which humanity is always landing. And, when Humanity lands there, it looks out, and seeing a better country, sets sail." In a more downbeat mood, one can say that a map of Ireland that does not include its elsewheres is not worth even glancing at, for it leaves out the places where Ireland is always landing and returning from.

The map of the world that illustrates Myles na Gopaleen's 1941 Irish language novel *An Béal Bocht (The Poor Mouth)* is thus as accurate as it is funny. Drawn by the artist Sean O'Sullivan, it represents "the great world as it appears to the people of Corca Dorcha," na Gopaleen's satiric peasant Ireland. In the middle is Ireland, an island with but a few features marked: Corca Dorcha, Sligo Jail, Dublin and Cork (containing "gentlefolk"), and a small piece towards the North marked "Orangemen". To the west is a similar sized island called *Thar Lear* (Overseas), which has long horn cattle, money order offices for emigrants' remittances, and three cities in the east: New York, Boston and Springfield, Mass. To the east, is a third island called *De Odar Saighd*, which has money order offices, George Bernard Shaw and a long bit at the top containing a money order office and a section marked "Gaelic spoken here," reached by routes marked "pratie hokers' routes". The compass on the map has four directions: West, West, West and West.

The book's other illustration, set in the text, is The Sea Cat, the terrible monster that assails the hero in one of his darkest hours. Unable to describe it in words, he draws it on a piece of paper. It is an outline map of Ireland on its side, the four great peninsulas of the west coast underneath as legs, Ulster a head, Wexford the tail. He is told that it is a horrible creature that comes ashore only to do evil, and that no one has seen it before and lived. The map of Ireland has become a comically monstrous creature, appearing now and then from the waves of the Atlantic, bringing nothing but misfortune in its wake.

The real map of such a place is etched into faces, since only the personal histories of emigrants accurately describe it. Eugene O'Neill, in his final reckoning with his emigrant past, *Long Day's Journey Into Night*, has his father's alter ego James Tyrone snap at his son, who has been bad-mouthing Ireland, "keep your dirty tongue off Ireland! You're a fine one to sneer, with the map of it on your face!" That map imprinted on a face, whose contours shift with smiles and frowns, is the most truthful map of Ireland there is.

Another such image is that near the end of Sam Shepard's play *A Lie of the Mind*. Two women, mother and daughter, are adrift in the modern American wilderness. They are preparing to set out and leave their lives behind, one sorting through old letters and photographs to decide what is junk, the other leafing through travel brochures. Suddenly the mother holds up a "big colourful map of Ireland," points to it and exclaims "I found it. Here it is. Right here. Sligo County. Connaught." She remembers a name — "Skellig. Mary Skellig, and there was a Shem or Sham or somethin' like that." — but she has never been to the place. Her only knowledge of it is that "I used to remember my grandma talk about it." The Skelligs are "Relatives. Ancestors. I don't know." Maybe, her daughter suggests, they are all dead. "People don't just all die. They don't just all up and die at once unless it's a catastrophe or somethin'. Someone's always left behind to carry on." And out of this vague sense that someone must be left behind, on the basis of this map of an unknown country, they stake their future on a trip to Ireland.

Between these two images of the map of Ireland — an indelible stain of the past on the face of the present, and a risky act of faith in the future — are the co-ordinates of the island on which we live. As an epigraph for his play Shepard chooses the words of Cesar Vallejo: "Something identifies you with the one who leaves you, and it is your common power to return: thus your greatest sorrow. Something separates you from the one who remains with you, and it is your common slavery to depart: thus your meagerest rejoicing." Between that going away and that remaining, the map of Ireland is stretched.

Shepard's image is more than fiction. The Irish folklorist, Seamus O Catháin, working in a farming community in Wisconsin, met a woman who told him a story. When she was a girl, a neighbour of hers had a single word written on the side of his barn. To her, the word was a dumb hieroglyph, letters and shapes without meaning. It had no known connotation or significance. Years later, when she was a grown woman, she came to Ireland on a visit. There, by chance, she came across the word again — BELMULLET — and realised for the first time that it was a place-name. It had stood on the side of that Wisconsin barn, a word without a meaning, a signifier in search of a signified, a placename without a place. Only now did it take on a content.

Such shadow placenames are part of the Irish map. The poet Ciaran Carson came across another in New York: "On an almost blank wall where East 46th Street intersects Avenue A in the area called Alphabet City in New York, New York, is the grafitto in three-foot-high black letters, saying BELFAST, with the cross-stroke of the T extended into an arrow pointing east, to Belfast. I have a photograph to prove this, but it's lost. In New York, no one that I ask seems to know the meaning of this careful scrawl, whether it's a gang, the code-word of a gang, a fashion, a club, or the name of the city where I was born; but the latter seems unlikely, though Alphabet City — barricaded liquor stores, secretive tobacco shops and elaborate Russian Orthodox churches — resembles Belfast, its roads pocked and skid-marked, littered with broken glass and crushed beer cans."

3.

In the Tipperary Inn in Montauk, Long Island, there are three maps of Ireland on the walls. None of them gives you much of a guide to the present geography of the place. One of them is a 50-year old map of a place called Eire, a schoolroom diagram in pastel colours of the mountain ranges and rivers that we learned off by heart and carried around in our heads like irregular verbs from an obscure and half-forgotten language. The second is a map of Literary Ireland. By definition, it is the map of a series of inventions, the places of writers, though if you know how to read it it may reveal something, since a map of the birthplaces of historic writers is also a map of absences, of places that these writers left behind.

The third map is still more fictional: a Genealogical Map of Ireland, its territories defined by the homes of tribes that were broken centuries ago, its borders decorated by the absurd crests and coats-of-arms that they borrowed from their conquerors centuries later in order to convince themselves that they had not, after all, been broken.

If none of these maps gives you much sense of direction, neither does the green street sign that hangs by the door: "Sraid Aonrai/Henry Street". In this context, Henry Street, that tunnel of cheeky charlies and wrapping paper, might be the name of a famous Irishman, or even a famous American. Hanging from the ceiling are three golden letters that are all that remains of what was once a banner: HAP... Happy Birthday? Happy Thanksgiving? Happy Saint Patrick's Day? The Ireland that is being celebrated here is a bit like that banner: the tattered remains of something that must have been wonderful if anyone could remember what it was.

The clock in the Tipperary Inn is entirely innocent of the right time, but it is getting very late. Shuffling around the dance floor to the sound of a band playing sixties hits are a few tanned American holiday makers. They have spent the day pretending to be Ernest Hemingway, hunting striped bass or vast tuna fish from the charter boats, and now they want a few beers and a stretch on the floor. Yet, if you're Irish there is something surreal about the way Ireland, or a version of Ireland, can be a holiday destination even in New York State. You can visit a little bit of Ireland without ever leaving America.

What is even more surreal is that you visit America without ever really leaving Ireland. Every shop, every bar, every hotel in Montauk seems to be staffed by young Irish people. You walk in feeling hip in your shades and shorts, only to be asked in familiar tones: "What's the weather like at home?" You have to think for a moment where home might be when a whole generation seems to be over here. There are so many Irish over here that that they have their own acronyms: as well as Yuppies and Dinkies, there are Biffos — Big Ignorant Fuckers From Offaly.

Anyway, it's very late in the Tipperary Inn, and the main entertainment is watching the last couple still on the dancefloor, him all muscles and shapes, her twice his age, done up to the nineteens, fretfully buying him drinks. It looks like it will soon be closing time.

Except that, for the Irish it is now opening time. Bit by bit, they start to drift in, two or three at a time until the place is full again. They are all of an age — early to mid twenties — and they are all of a mind to enjoy themselves. You realise that, whereas, for the tourists, this is the fag-end of the day, for the Irish it is the beginning, the time when work has ended and the fun can start. The shops they work in have closed, the night staff have come on duty in the hotels. Soon, the Americans will start to drift off to bed, leaving the place to the real natives, the people who work and make a life here, the Irish.

Not that this Irish life is settled. The tourist season is coming to a close and most of the Irish will have to move on, back to New York or Boston, or out West, or, if things are really slack, back to Mullingar and Dublin, Roscommon and Wexford. You meet the odd Irish person who works year-round on the fishing boats or the restaurants, but most are migratory emigrants, doubly unsettled, following the work. Tonight, some of the Irish have had a barbecue on the beach to say goodbye to each other. Their temporary communities resolve and dissolve themselves. Yet in the shifting, permanently temporary society of America, this is no big deal. The Irish here still seem like the consistent presence around which things revolve, the natives who have things better sussed, who know the ins and outs. These emigrants seem to define the place.

And some of them, the lucky ones who have Green Cards and university degrees, will become more and more settled with time. The wedding has now replaced the wake as the symbol of the permanence of emigration. Before, the American Wake, held on the night before the journey to Cobh for the boat, was the recognition that the emigrant was passing away to another side, probably forever. You still meet older Irish immigrants in America who talk about "the other side," meaning Ireland, as if emigration were a passage through the borders between one state of existence and another. But for the younger generation, who went to America young, free and single, it is the act of marrying in America that now marks the real passage to the other side, the final statement that home is no longer

24

a place that you visit at Christmas time, but the place in which you put up the Christmas tree for your children.

To settle down is also to settle accounts, to draw a line under the transaction called "Ireland," accept the losses and gains, and begin to define yourself as American. It is preferable to the never-ending cycle of emigration and return, to the fate of having to shift your country with every boom and recession, which is becoming, for more and more people, the reality.

And so, on the dancefloor of the Tipperary Inn, under the auspices of three fictional maps of Ireland, the standard courtship rituals of the young have a special edge. The vague possibilities that always hover around a dancefloor, the possibilities of permanent links being formed, of families and generations arising out of this madcap revels, of somebody, somewhere, having a memory that their grandparents met on this floor, seem poignantly distant. Because some of them are illegal aliens, because many have just marked their departure from this place, because their lives are cast on the waters of uncertainty, how could a glimmer of the future ever break through those dancing eyes? If this were Ireland, and not just a maze of untrustworthy maps, at this hour the barman would long ago have asked "Have yis no homes to go to?" But it isn't and they haven't.

In a country where the places and their names will not stick together because the places and their people have not stuck together, maps have to be descriptions of the imagination, of memory and desire, as well as of physical terrain. The most potent Irish maps of recent years, those of the Aran Islands and the Burren by Tim Robinson, are records, not merely of topography, but of the people he met, the stories he was told, while making them. Of his Aran map, Robinson wrote that he "tried to see Aran through variously informed eyes — and then, alone again, I have gone hunting for those rare places and times, the nodes at which the layers of experience touch and may be fused together. But I find that in a map such points and the energy that accomplishes such fusions... can, at most, be invisible guides, benevolent ghosts, through the tangles of the explicit; they cannot themselves be shown or named." This sense that a map-maker has that there are ghosts behind the explicit, that the recorded details of the map owe much to what cannot be named or acknowledged seems the only spirit in which a map of Ireland is possible. When Belfast is a mysterious graffito on a New York wall and Belmullet an inarticulate jumble of letters on the side of a Wisconsin barn, hidden presences and charged absences must haunt the maps we make.

4.

"The unsettling of a nation is an easy work, the settling is not."

— Vincent Gookin, *The Great Case of Transplantation in Ireland,* 1655

Emigration, all-embracing as it is, is not the only force that belies the map of Ireland. There is a sense in which even the points of the compass are no longer fixed in Irish experience. Ireland ought to be one of the most clearly defined of public spaces. It is a bounded entity if ever there was one: a small island at the outer limit of one continent, Europe, and facing, across thousands of miles of ocean, another, America. But this is a trick of the eye, an illusion which tantalises the reality of a place that is permeable, that on the one hand seems connnected to too many conflicting loyalties of place and on the other seems to melt away into the sea, as if the coastline that surrounds the country were merely a thin membrane that lets in all the flotsam and jetsam of consumer culture and lets out a constant flow of people and capital. On the one hand, in the North, there is no agreement about what the political space is: the United Kingdom or a United Ireland? On the other, in the South, there is constant difficulty in maintaining a political space at all.

If you see a country as its people rather than its territory, then, far from being small and well-defined, Ireland has been, for at least 150 years, scattered, splintered, atomised like the windscreen of a crashed car. In 1990, the population of Ireland was about the same as it was in 1890 after decades of famine, violence and mass emigration. All the natural increase in the meantime had been lost to emigration. Ireland is a diaspora, and as such is both a real place and a remembered place, both the far west of Europe and the home back east of the Irish-American. Ireland is something that often happens elsewhere. And this is both a cause and a consequence of its sense of being an unstable place, a place all the time having to struggle to become a political entity. A cause because emigration makes the borders of the island permeable. A consequence because, when you grow up in a country which it is hard to imagine as a political entity, then equally it is hard to imagine a way in which you might help to change that place. Change becomes personal, not political: you change your location, not your society.

In such a place, neither internal boundaries nor external co-ordinates hold their meaning. Even the most unconscious of boundaries, the old county divisions, separating one political constituency and, more importantly, one county hurling or football team, from another, are often uneasy and artificial. One of the most rooted of Irish writers, one of the most certain of his sense of place is John McGahern, yet he has this to say about his native Leitrim: "Except for football and politics, the county divisions mean little to the people. For those who live on the Shannon, North Leitrim might as well be Cornwall. It is each single, enclosed locality that matters and everything that happens within it is of passionate interest to those who live there. Do you have any news, any news? But once that news crosses a certain boundary, eyes that a moment before were wild with curiosity will suddenly glaze. News no longer local is of no interest." More and more the boundaries are private and familial rather than public and political.

On the mental map of Ireland now, unlike the mental map in *An Béal Bocht* where all directions are one, the compass tends to point in all directions at once. Geography is a politics as much as it is a science. For Northern Protestants, Britain is the mainland, as if Northern Ireland were the Isle of Man. For Northern Catholics, West Belfast, although it is in the east of the island, is part of the West, because the West, for over a century now, has been the symbol of pure, Catholic, native Ireland, and West Belfast wants to belong to that symbolism. Donegal, which is at the northern boundary of the island, is in the south, because it is part of the Republic. In Dublin, North and South are not points on the compass, but social categories, the Northside supposedly working-class, the Southside supposedly middle-class, that allow the embarrassing subject of class division to be alluded to without being openly acknowledged. Direction is a matter of psychological orientation. History, not geography, defines the space you inhabit.

These contortions of north and south are now matched, and to an extent bypassed, by the other shifting axis of east and west. In Irish nationalist mythology, the West was the locus of the real Ireland, and the goal of politics was to make the whole country as like the West as possible. In reality, though, the West was marginalised economically and culturally, poorer, less populous, more vulnerable to the loss of its people through emigration. And, in the Single European Market, this double association of the West with romantic aspirations and with actual marginality is catching up with the country as a whole.

It has become hard for Irish politicians to decide whether their country is East or West. Albert Reynolds, the Taoiseach, told *The Irish Times* in November, 1992 that his

28

ambition was "to link the Americas with Europe and to make Ireland the bridgehead in that link from west to east." A bridgehead is a fortified military position held on the enemy's side of a natural barrier. So Ireland becomes a piece of Europe captured by America, a piece of America captured by Europe. It becomes neither east nor west, but some kind of embattled border zone.

Or consider a map of Ireland in Europe from *Manager-Magazin*, a glossy German business publication, of March 1990. The heading on the map is "Boom, Boom, Boom: European growth in the 1990s". Central and western Europe are shown with new divisions to replace the old borders. A banana-shaped "North-South axis" encloses an area from the English South through Holland and Belgium, south-western Germany, Switzerland and Northern Italy. A new country called Sunbelt runs from Lyon through the Côte d'Azur, Catalonia and the north-eastern corner of Spain. And a thick blue line to the west of the map, arcing gracefully to the west of Scotland but east of Ireland, down through much of Wales and the West Country, through Britanny and the west of Spain, invents a new place called "Atlantik -Peripherie". The only full country in it is Ireland, coloured a bold grey-green as are southern Spain and Sardinia and the South of Italy. Though we do not know it, this is where we live now.

For what the West of Ireland was to the rest of the country, Ireland as a whole, North and South, now is to the rest of the European union: a romantic but backward periphery. The majority of the population which lives on the eastern half of the island has been used to thinking of itself as East, not West. Now, in the context of the EU, it has to think of itself as West, not East. On the scale of Europe, most of the country is a western margin, what the German map calls "the Atlantic periphery". In the hard white light of Euro-economics, space and place lose their romance and are reduced to a set of unpromising figures. Using an index of accessibility to European markets,

Ireland is defined as part of the outer periphery, the lowest in a five-category spatial classification. Its accessibility score, in which space is converted into money, is only 55 per cent of the average of all the regions of the EU. It is 21 per cent and 17 per cent respectively of the Rheinhessen-Pfalz and of London, which belong to the "core".

In this new understanding of public space, this new map, places are related to each other not by their proximity or by the fact that they form part of the same nation or state, but by the fact that they share the same degree of accessibility to markets. The outer periphery, to which Ireland belongs, is not a little island but the 40 per cent of the land area of the EU that has just 20 per cent of the population and 13 per cent of the Gross Domestic Product. Distance is economic, not physical: Edinburgh may be as far from the Rhine as Dublin is, but it is part of the core whereas Dublin is part of the outer periphery, simply because Edinburgh is more accessible and richer. In this sense, the new map of post-1992 Europe is one in which Dublin, and Belfast, are in the West, along with Warsaw, Bucharest and Lisbon, while Edinburgh and London are in the East along with Stuttgart and Nice and Rome. Where space is measured, not in miles or kilometres, but in marks or francs, it is hard to get your bearings.

It was, after all, another Irishman, Jonathan Swift, who invented, in *Gulliver's Travels*, the idea of a flying island, Laputa. Ireland is now a sort of flying island, hovering between a number of different contexts, often flying blind with no one too sure of how the controls work anymore. It touches down now in The Bronx, now in Bonn, now in Britain, seeking connections with a set of overlapping places, but always taking off again into its own outer spaces.

5.

"The word-world of Finnegans Wake has its own geography, and a very queer geography it is too, since it violates the geographical postulate of identification by fixed co-ordinates. Not only do the boundaries of Dublin expand to include the rest of the terrestrial globe and the indefinite loci of fiction and mythology, but the very dimensions of space itself become uncertainly elastic and transform themselves into one or more dimensions of time."

— Louis O. Mink, *A Finnegans Wake Gazeteer*

The geography of Ireland at the end of the 20th century is a version of the queer geography of Joyce's *Finnegans Wake*, in which Dublin is also the Dublin that is the county seat of Laurens County, Georgia; Baile Atha Cliath is also Balaclava; Dublin is also Lublin; the New Ireland is the New Island (America); Crumlin is the Kremlin; West Munster is Westminster, and the four provinces are the erogenous zones of "used her, mused her, licksed her and cuddled." Its proper maps are those searched for by the great cartographer Tim Robinson, seeking those "nodes at which the layers of experience touch and may be fused together."

They may be nothing more than the map in Miroslav Holub's poem *Brief Thoughts on Maps*. According to the poem, a young lieutenant in a Hungarian regiment during the First World War sent a reconnaissance unit out into the icy wastes of the Alps. Almost immediately they were engulfed in a blizzard and lost from view. When they had not returned for two days, the lieutenant, racked with guilt, realised that he had sent his own people to their deaths.

On the third day, however, the reconnaissance unit came back. They admitted that they had lost their way and that, in despair, they had slumped into the snow to await the end. Then, on a final check, one of them had found a map in his pocket. That calmed them down and gave them heart. They pitched camp, waited out the snowstorm, and then, with the map, found their bearings. And here they were. The lieutenant borrowed the map, and had a good look at it. It was a map, not of the Alps, but of the Pyrenees.

TOURISTS IN OUR OWN LAND

1.

There is a famous story by Jorge Luis Borges in which the Emperor becomes more and more obsessed with having a detailed map of his territory. As he becomes madder, and the cartographers work harder, they eventually come up with a map whose scale is one-to-one. The map is the same size as the territory and as it is spread out it covers the entire country. The landscape disappears under a detailed and precise map of itself. To this story we in Ireland have one refinement to offer. When the map is finally spread out over the landscape, we will build a few interpretative centres on it, so that visitors may be taught its meaning.

In all the debates about the plans by the Office of Public Works to build interpretative centres in the Burren, Wicklow and the Boyne Valley, debates that continued with increasing bitterness into 1994, one rather central question remained virtually unasked. The question is a simple enough one: what is there to interpret? There is no difficulty in the notion that people visiting a place can do with some information about it. But the very phrase "interpretative centre" implies something much more. It implies not information but meaning. It implies that a landscape can be interrogated for its meaning in the same way that a book or a play or a political statement can be. And this is a very profound implication to make. It marks a shift in the way we think about land and nature which we should not allow to happen without at least realising that it is happening.

Particularly in relation to the debate around the Mullaghmore centre, it can be said that the opposition lost the battle once it became possible to characterise it as the creature of high-minded intellectuals cut off from reality.

Yet what is interesting about this characterisation is that, not only is it untrue, it is the precise opposite of the truth. It is the whole function of interpretative centres to intellectualise reality, to turn nature into culture, to make a physical reality into a "meaning" and that meaning into a product. If there is an intellectual conceit at work, it is in the very notion of an interpretative centre, not in the opposition that that notion arouses.

If you visited Mullaghmore before the interpretative centre was there, even if you just got out of your car and looked at it, the last thing you would have wanted to do was to think much about it. Maybe, afterwards, when you got home, you might take out one of the excellent books on the Burren currently available and read about history and geology and morphology and flora and fauna. But that would have been something else, a different experience entirely. When you were there, when you were looking at the mountain, you would have felt it as something in itself, a thing outside of the world of reflection and meaning and interpretation that we all live in most of the time.

If you now move up the coast to Glenveigh National Park in Donegal, you find a place of equal beauty and wildness. But your first experience of it will be paying for your ticket at the gate. Then the drive up to the carpark. Then the carefully signposted route to the interpretative centre. Then the toilets, the maps, the displays, the audio-visual theatre, the restaurant. By the time you actually start to walk around the lake, it has become in some way a second-hand experience, a replay of a movie that is already running in your head. Just as, when you first visit New York, there is the disconcerting sense of having seen these streets a thousand times in movies and cop series, you get the feeling of something that is familiar even though you have never seen it before. The place is still beautiful, but it is no longer strange. It is a fine tourist product, a place that has been given a commercially viable meaning. It has been interpreted.

There is, of course, nothing unique about what is going on in Ireland in this respect. But it is going on in a virtually unique, or at least very particular way.

Ways of treating the landscape have always been connected to the way an economy is organised. A peasant society always looks differently at the land out of which it ekes an existence than an industrial society does. For one, it is a means of making a living. For the other it is a means of escaping the means by which you make a living, a relief from cities and offices and factories. Modern societies have their own way of looking at landscape, making it precious and strange and even holy. But as modern societies become post-modern ones, as industrial cultures become post-industrial ones, this too changes. In societies based on image-making, societies in which everything — sex, nature, James Dean's look, Marilyn Monroe's wiggle — has become a commodity, landscape is just one more commodity, one manufactured image among others.

What is peculiar about Ireland is that we have become a post-modern society without ever fully becoming a modern one. We have gone from the few hungry acres to the Financial Services Centre with only a half-finished project of modernity in between. We have a society in which a husband and wife will go jail over a few acres of bog (as happened in 1992), and at the same time a society in which landscape is a distant, emotion-free object to be "interpreted". The middle bit, the bit where landscape is a strange and sacred thing, is missing. Or at least it is present only in the half-developed form of a half-modern-ised society.

What we end up with is a landscape that is so strange that it has to be interpreted for us, but not strange enough to be accorded the wary reverence that we give to the genuinely unknown. If we were still peasants, we wouldn't think twice about building a whole village on the top of Mullaghmore if we had the money and the reason to do it. Yet, if we were fully Los Angelised, we wouldn't think twice about turning it completely into a product. Instead of putting the interpretative centre near the mountain, we would happily shift the mountain to be near the interpretative centre. But as it is, we are somehere in the middle between these states of mind, conscious enough of the strangeness of these places to want to control them, to put a frame of ordinariness around them, but not conscious enough of it to be able to leave them be. We offer a place like Mullaghmore the kind of interpretation that reduces it while pretending to honour it.

We give it a kind of pseudo-meaning. Far from there being intellectuals who oppose interpretative centres on the one side and "real" people on the other side who want them, the whole notion of the interpretative centre can be seen as the product of an over-active mind, a mind that must always substitute meaning for experience. We can't experience the landscape as our peasant grandparents did. And we can't discard that experience as our grandchildren (for whom it will have no more meaning than James Dean's eyebrows or Marilyn Munroe's hips, another image among images) will when they fly in from Los Angeles or Berlin to our theme parks. So we try to replace the experience with a meaning.

Susan Sontag wrote well about this desire for interpretation nearly 30 years ago. "Today," she wrote, "the project of interpretation is largely reactionary, stifling. Like the fumes of the automobile and of heavy industry which befoul the urban atmosphere, the effusion of interpretations...today poisons our sensibilities. Interpretation is the revenge of the intellect upon the world. To interpet is to impoverish, to deplete the world — in order to set up a shadow world of 'meanings'. It is to turn the world into *this* world."

We need interpreters only when we are away from home and the language is not ours. To hire an interpreter is to admit that we cannot be spoken to directly. It is an acknowledgement of incomprehension. The rash of interpretative centres is the first public admission that we are now abroad in Ireland, that we have become tourists in our own land.

2.

Recently, a member of the West Wicklow Historical Society, Mrs Dorothy Leonard, spotted three particular old headstones in the Church of Ireland churchyard in Clonmelsh, County Carlow. One of them belonged to a certain Robert Disney, who married Mary Keppel at the Carlow Church of Ireland parish church in 1775, and who died in Kilkenny city in 1808. The discovery of this tombstone was apposite in its timing, for it confirmed what many of us in Ireland have been coming to suspect in recent years. Robert and Mary were the great, great, great grandparents of Walter Elias Disney, better known as Walt, and therefore the great, great, great, great grandparents of Michael Mouse, Donald Duck and James, alias Jiminy, Cricket. *Irish Roots*, the magazine for genealogists, reported the discovery under the headline MICKEY MOUSE IS IRISH. Disneyland has discovered its roots and is coming home.

Many great national or tribal epics — think, for instance, of the *Book of Chronicles* in the *Old Testament*, or of Gabriel Garcia Marquez's *One Hundred Years of Solitude* which begin with genealogies, and if contemporary Ireland were to have a national epic, it should begin with this one. Robert and Mary begat Keppel, Keppel begat Arundal Elias, Arundal Elias begat the second Keppel, the second Keppel begat Elias, Elias begat Walter Elias, Walter Elias begat Mickey and Minnie. Mickey and Minnie begat Disneyland. And Disneyland begat a new tourist Ireland, a land of re-created "heritage" and forgotten history, of interpretative centres and lost meanings, of a post-modern hyper-reality sitting side-by-side with a not yet fully modern society.

This genealogy which is real and unreal at the same time, based in recorded fact, yet expressing the surrealism of Ireland's participation in postmodern media culture, is typical of what critical theory has come to recognise, in Frederic Jameson's phrase, as "postmodern fantastic historiography, as that is found alike in wild imaginary genealogies and novels that shuffle historical figures and names like so many cards from a finite deck." The fact that it is found in a typical Irish tourist product — *Irish Roots* magazine — and not in an avant garde novel is, in a sense, the point of the essay.

What I want to draw attention to here is the way in which mass tourism is beginning to literally shape the landscape of Ireland in a way which arises from precisely the same forces that shape contemporary fiction and poetry and contemporary critical theory. Bord Failte and the Office of Public Works do not, so far as I know, read Derrida and Baudrillard, or even Gabriel Garcia Marquez and E.L Doctorow, but they are themselves fabulists and makers of simulacra, creators of their own post-modern school. The difference is that their fables actually and literally change the world.

The best place to start is with Frederic Jameson's admirable definition of the post-modern :

"Postmoderism is what you have when the modernisation process is complete and nature is gone for good. It is a more fully human world than the older one, but one in which 'culture' has become a veritable 'second nature'. Indeed what happened to culture may well be one of the more important clues for tracking the postmodern: an immense dilation of its sphere, an immense and historically original acculturation of the Real, a quantum leap in what Benjamin still called the 'aestheticization' of reality."

This great leap forward in the processing of nature into culture is what I will call postmodern here. And it is clear even from that short definition that what has happened in

Irish tourism, most sharply in the debate over Mullaghmore, is about more than just the best place to put toilets for tour buses. It is about the relationship of Ireland to that totality of contemporary culture that is called postmodern. It is about whether, in Ireland, the completion of the modernisation process is, indeed, the death of nature, the final triumph of culture over landscape.

This question presents itself to most people in a local, specific way. It is a question of whether this road should be widened for tour buses, whether this field should be levelled and a new building be put on it, whether these plants and these rocks will be threatened, whether my Mary might get a job selling postcards and serving coffee, so that she might not have to emigrate. What does not present itself to most people is how literary this process is, how much it is a self-conscious attempt to construct narratives, to tell stories, to present for the consumer the perfect post-modern range of alternative histories, which can be chosen, mixed, reversed, quoted, made into a collage of reality and fantasy at will.

The blueprint for the interpretative centres built in Ireland over the first few years of the 1990s is contained in a report drawn up for Bord Failte in 1990 by a firm of consultants in England, and revised in 1992 in a Bord Failte document called *Heritage Attractions Development: a strategy to interpret Ireland's history and culture for tourism*. The latter starts with a problem: the complexity of that history and that culture:

"While the folk culture of Ireland is relatively easily appreciated, Irish history, due to the influence of many peoples, cultures and conflicts, is not easily understood by visitors... Many visitors arrive with a limited awareness of a few elements of this heritage, but there is little common ground to start further exploration. Visitors' time is also limited, and in many cases is predetermined by tour operators, so it is important to help increase visitors' understanding by creating interpretative 'gateways' into our heritage. This will heighten their experience, increase satisfaction levels and help in awareness and appreciation of individual sites, the end result will be more repeat business, better 'word of mouth' publicity and the creation of a strong 'brand image' of Ireland as a quality heritage destination, with unique heritage attractions."

The gateways are narratives, stories. Everything is to be understood as part of a particular storyline, and "it is proposed that all storylines be clustered around five key themes": live landscapes, making a living, saints and religion, building a nation and the spirit of Ireland. Thirty storylines clustered around these themes are suggested, but it is stressed that "new storylines are possible under all of the themes." Thus, eventually, all landscape, all culture, all history, will become part of a single timeless and placeless grid of stories into which the tourist can tap in the same way that a computer user can tap into a databank.

In this self-conscious spinning out of story-lines, history and geography are conflated. On the one hand, landscape is no longer to be understood as a function of place or space, but is to be aestheticised into a narrative, a story. It ceases to be geography and becomes history. But equally, history becomes a function of geography. The grid of stories is designed to be plugged into on a journey around Ireland by the tourist. Time and space, in other words, become mixed up together. History is suspended in a commodifed sense of place. This indeed may be the essence of tourism itself, but it is also characteristic of postmodern culture, of which Jameson notes that:

"It must also be considered a spatial phenomenon in the most fundamental sense, since, whatever the provenance of the various items combined in their postmodern incompatability — whether they stem from different zones of time or from unrelated compartments of the social and material universe — it is their spatial separation that is strongly felt as such. Different moments in historical or existential time are here simply filed in different places; the attempt to combine them even locally does not slide up and down a temporal scale... but jumps back and forth across a game board that we conceptualise in terms of distance. Thus the movement from one generic classification to another is radically discontinuous, like switching channels on a cable television set."

This general description of postmodern methodology exactly matches Bord Failte's master plan for "interpreting Ireland's history and culture for tourism". There is the same filing of historical and existential moments in different compartments, like supermarket shelves from which the tourist can fill a basket of memories at random, the same jumping back and forth across the game board, the same channel hopping. And the two are aspects of the same phenomenon — the loss of history. The making up of unreal history is, as Jameson says, a substitute for the making of the real kind. "Fabulation — or, if you prefer, mythomania and outright tall tales — is no doubt a symptom of social and historical impotence, of the blocking of possibilities that leaves little option but the imaginary." It is a function of "a new and original historical situation in which we are condemned to seek History by way of our own pop images and simulacra of that history, which itself remains forever out of reach."

And in Ireland, there is a specific shape to this general phenomenon. The grand narrative of Irish nationalist history has been destroyed, leaving a gap for the pop images to fill, not merely for the tourist but for the native as well. In the process, the real relationship of history and geography, the real narrative of this landscape, is occluded. That narrative is a paradoxical one in which Famine and depopulation have made an empty landscape that tourists can come for. The stones of what were once houses have fallen into the stones of the fields. The gable walls of famine cottages have been over-grown with foliage. The landscape has re-claimed human settlement. The pleasure

41

of its emptiness is founded on human catastrophe. In this regard, the interpretation of the landscape has much to hide.

In relation to the landscape, the process of postmodernisation really does complete an aspect of the modern project, though in a way which is opposite to the intentions of those who set it in motion. One of the most radical aspects of the early Romantic movement was the attempt to replace history painting and epic poetry with landscape. They wished to make pure landscape without figures carry the weight, attain the heroic significance, of historical painting or of the epic style of Homer or Milton. Landscape was to be the vehicle of the Sublime. The Romantics believed that the simplest forms of Nature could speak directly to us, could express sentiments and ideas without the intervention of culture. Landscape, they believed, could be forged into a language without conventions, a universally intelligible form of expression that would be not discursive but evocative.

They reckoned without two things. One was the impossibility of a language, even a language of landscapes, that was not, in the end conventional, as all languages, by their very nature are. They looked to nature as an escape from culture, but inevitably created a culture of nature. The other thing they reckoned without was tourism. What tourism did was to make the experience they thought of as single and unequivocal subject to a constant double vision. Tourism meant that the images of the wilderness created by Romantic artists could be brought back to that wilderness by travellers who would see nature precisely through those images. The Honourable John Byng, the English traveller in Wales in the 1790s, complained that the engravers of mass produced landscape prints should also provide sketch maps to help the tourist get to the place in the picture.

On the Celtic fringes of which Ireland is a part this process happened first and most clearly in Wales, which had both the necessary romantic scenery and the easy accessibility from industrial Britain, the good roads which allowed Wordsworth to climb Mount Snowdon without too much bother and be followed by a tourist industry. Welsh literature produces almost no descriptions of landscape before the nineteenth century, and those that there are are to do with property, human activity, produce, skill, work, but not beauty. The Welsh themselves thought of their landscape of mountains and stones, in the words of historian Prys Morgan, as "a punishment meted out by the Almighty to the Welsh for past sins." One English tourist, the Reverend William Bingley, recalled being constantly asked had he no rocks or waterfalls in his own country.

In the 1750s and 1760s, the Welsh Romantic painter Richard Wilson began to paint the mountains in the genuine Romantic spirit of wonder, but he was notably unsuccessful and died in obscurity in 1782. Within a few years, however, tourism from England had started, inspired by the new Romanticism. and Wilson's paintings were reproduced and copied in their thousands. One of waterfalls which he had painted became known as "Wilson's pool". The landscape, through the combination of romanticism and tourism, was becoming almost literally aestheticised.

And this process became narrative as well as pictorial. Having acquired a pictorial quality, the landscape began to acquire stories. In the 1790s, a hotelier in Beddgelert invented the legend that the village took its name from the burial cairn of Gelert, the favorite hound of Prince Llywelyn the Great, whom he had unjustly killed. Since there was no burial mound, he went out quietly and built it. Tourists flocked to the spot. Poems were written about it. Haydn set one of the poems to music. Within a few years, the story had found its way into native Welsh-speaking culture and had become a traditional Welsh-language tale about the local landscape. The landscape now was the story told about it.

In Ireland, broadly the same process has unfolded, but it has happened more recently and in a more clearly politicised way than in Wales. Here, too, the people who lived in the landscape were more inclined to think of it as a curse and a punishment, which, with the Cromwellian displacement of population, it really was, than as a thing of beauty. There are no awestruck descriptions of landscape in the writings of the Blasket Island writers of the 1920s. In fact, their awe is reserved for the products of the industrial revolution. Tomas O' Crohan, in his diary of Blasket life published in English as *Island Cross-Talk*, records a day in October 1922 which is the nearest the islanders come to a holiday, a day when no work is done, no dinner is eaten, because all are wrapt in wonder, watching big ships "ploughing the ocean through a storm... the smoke from every funnel rising to the clouds." He notes that "one was so vast that you would think a mountain had collapsed into the sea every time she dipped her nose downwards." Mountains of steel and smoke, not mountains of stone and water, were their source of wonder and awe, their holiday from the quotidian.

This reality was obscured by the political rhetoric of militant Irish nationalism which was deeply Romantic and which saw in landscape the true guarantee of the nation's purity and distinctiveness. In Patrick Pearse's rhetoric, for instance:

"The Gael is the high priest of nature. He loves nature, not merely as something grand and beautiful and wonderful but as something possessing a mystic connection with and influence over man. In the cry of the seagull as he winged his solitary flight over the Atlantic waves; in the shriek of the eagle as he wheeled around the heights of the Kerry mountains; in the note of the throstle as he sang his evening lay in the woods of Slieve Grot; in the roar of the cataract as it foamed and splashed down the rocky ravine; in the sob of the ocean as it beat unceasingly against the cliffs of Achill; in the sign of the wind as it moved, ghost-like, through the oaks of Derrybawn — in all these sounds the ancient Gael heard a music unheard by other men."

This very Romanticism of Irish political nationalism was itself a part of the process of the recreation of nature as culture, and Pearse himself played a curious role in that process:

"Once Padraig brought down a cinematograph operator to Connemara and gave an entertainment in an adjacent school. But first of all he provided a plentiful supply of barn-bracks and sweets for the children. It was the first time that anything like it had ever been seen in the district and many funny remarks were passed thereon. One old woman tried hard to get behind the screen to see the real people! Her remarks should be quoted in Irish in order to give the real full value. Padraig had beautiful rural scenes shown."

The process of making people observers of their own lives, audiences for their own culture, tourists of their own landscapes had been set in train.

3.

What is tourism for? For making money, of course. For providing jobs, of course. But those are by-products, economic benefits derived from an activity that is about something else. No weary German executive, no enthusiastic American matron, is suddenly possessed, come June, of an irresistible desire to sustain a job in County Clare, to help the Irish balance of payments, to contribute to the serene reconciliation of a hotelier's bank account. Tourism is no more motivated by economic growth than the beef industry is fuelled by a desire to make Larry Goodman rich. People buy beef because they need to eat; they buy holidays to satisfy some more nebulous, but no less insistent demand in their own natures.

45

Yet we insist on talking about tourism as if it were, first and foremost, about jobs and money. The debate on Mullaghmore, which is essentially a debate about tourism, is conducted entirely in these terms. It is a truth universally acknowledged in the marketplace that the providers of products who think only in their own terms, and not in those of their customers, who do not constantly worry about why people want their products, go bust. This truth has, however, been largely ignored in the consideration of interpretative centres.

There is a good reason for this reticence. The question is not asked because it is a hard question to answer, at least in terms of economic considerations. We are talking about an activity that, from the point of view of the consumer, makes no sense. Tourism is a useless endeavour, an immense amount of activity undertaken for no palpable gain. And, of course, it is its very uselessness, the quality of its irrationality, that is its point. A holiday is good in inverse proportion to its resemblance to our everyday economic activities.

Yet the issues raised by Mullaghmore are so fundamental, and the conflict over it so powerfully symbolic in both political and social terms, that it is time to ask these very basic questions. In doing so, we trespass on notions of wonder, adventure, and fantasy — not notions normally allowed into public debate, but ones which are essential when we are dealing, as with Mullaghmore, with the vague desires of travellers and the sense of identity of the natives.

It is not that long ago that we did actually think of tourism as having a moral, as well as an economic purpose. After the Second World War, Eamon de Valera spoke of Ireland's aim to "bind up some of the gaping wounds of suffering humanity," and there was actually a sense in the 1950s that the quietness and peace of Ireland could, by helping to heal those wounds for tourists, make up in some way for our neutrality during the war. Michael

O'Loughlin's poem *Heinrich Böll in Ireland* expresses it best:

Later, some stumbled across our shores

In search of a green poultice

For wounds we couldn't have understood.

There, at last, a small destiny, ours.

The notion, though, was prone to easy abuse, and could not survive the airy waffling of its friends, who used it to make a virtue of Ireland's poverty and backwardness and to construct a new, obscurantist version of the "spiritual empire". The playwright Paul Vincent Carroll, for instance, wrote in 1954 that "it may well be that Ireland will never become either populous or prosperous like Denmark or Belgium. She may well be destined to be the saviour of idealism in a world jungle of rank material weeds, and perhaps distracted foreigners, driven to despair by the ever-multiplying complexities of a machine- and gadget-ridden age, will visit her to try to re-learn ... the unutterable simplicities of living."

Guff like that discredited the very notion that we might actually be able to offer something to tourists as well as taking more tangible things from them. Another poet, Patrick Kavanagh, caught, in *The Great Hunger*, the savage irony of tourists watching the man trapped in his field from which there is "no escape, no escape," and vapourising about the peasant as the root of civilisation, before moving on, as he cannot,

The travellers touch the roots of the grass and feel

 renewed

When they grasp the steering wheels again.

The people of the Burren would rather have jobs than be left as embodiments of the unutterable simplicities of living, and the undoubted local anger at oposition to the Mullaghmore interpretative centre has a long history behind it. Nobody wants to have to live out somebody else's holiday fantasy, to be the saviour of idealism because you can't afford the materialism that everybody else lives by. They would rather be Denmark or Belgium, and who can blame them?

Yet, the fact remains that the people who will go to look at Mullaghmore now are not O'Crohan's people, or Patrick Kavanagh's people. They are not people for whom a ship is a more wondrous mountain than a mountain is. They are not people who, like Kavanagh's neighbours, will look at a mountain and ask *"Who owns them hungry hills / That the water-hen and snipe must have forsaken?"* and conclude that *"by heavens he must be poor."* They are urbanised people like me. Just as a peasant might look at a ship and think it a mountain, they are people who will look at a mountain and think it a ship, a transport to a new world of wonderment, not a piece of poor ground.

If it is to bring any economic benefit at all, Mullaghmore must remain capable of being this for people who will come to see it. It must remain essentially different from their everyday experience. It must be seen in terms of their lives, not of the lives of the people who live around the mountain and take it for granted. That may seem unfair and oppressive, but it is the price of making the mountain a tourist attraction. If it is to yield its economic by-products, jobs and money, it has to be thought of in terms other than economic ones.

The paradox can best be approached by saying that the aim of good tourism is to produce a sense of loss. It is to create a sense of regret on the part of those who have to move on, back to their everyday world. The essential irrationality of tourism is that we pay a lot of money in order to be profoundly dissatisfied, to be reminded that that there are things which, in the repetitions of everyday life, we are missing.

A holiday is about, not so much passing the time, as making time pass. In our everyday lives, time doesn't really pass. Everything comes round again. The sameness of the days means that everything repeats itself, and something which you didn't do yesterday can be done today. Small children don't have this notion, which is why a three year-old will protest bitterly at being hauled away from the playground, even though you insist that he was there yesterday and will be there again tomorrow.

We go to the trouble and expense of holidays to become three year-olds again, to experience the sense of being hauled away from something which we cannot return to every day. The search of the tourist is not for different places, but for a different sense of time, for moments of time that are present and then gone, rather than for the endlessly returning moments which make up our daily lot.

This is why interpretative centres are so misconceived. They present the experience of a place precisely as being infinitely repeatable. They define the experience and offer it again and again, day in, day out, throughout the season. They seek to satisfy, when the quest is for a form of dissatisfaction, to offer a calculable gain, when the search is for a sense of loss. They treat tourists as rational consumers rather than what they are — consumers of the irrational.

We should remember that sustainable tourism development — and the economic benefits that flow from it — depends on offering the tourist something as well as taking something away from the tourist. What Mullaghmore offers is the capacity to create moments that are at odds with everyday experience. Without that capacity, which will be greatly diminished by the interpretative centre, it is just another hungry hill. And hungry hills won't feed the Burren's children.

The process which is currently underway is best summed up in a story which the writer Niall Williams, who lives in rural Clare, told me recently. He went to a meeting of locals in the most western peninsula of Clare, a place that is dying because it is off the tourist trail. The meeting had been called to try to think up ways in which tourism might be brought to the area. One old man got up at the

49

back and made a suggestion. It had struck him that many tourists wanted to visit the Holy Land, but that most, particularly Americans, would be afraid to do so because of political unrest and the fear of terrorism. It has also struck him that this part of Clare had hills and seas, and rivers and plenty of space.

So, it seemed to him, the solution was obvious: they must re-create the Holy Land in the West Clare peninsula. The towns and villages would be re-named as Bethlehem, Nazareth, Bethseda. Goleen Bay would become the Shores of Galillee. Borges's emperor's map would become a reality, except with an added twist of strangeness: the map laid out on the landscape would be a map of another place altogether. Niall Williams told me that what amazed him was not so much the proposal as the fact that no one was amazed by it. People listened and nodded. It was noted in the minutes. Such is the desperation for tourism, as the only way of keeping places alive, that the reality of such people can only be preserved by making it into a hyper-reality. Instead of Disneyland we will have Holy Land, an original Irish contribution to the theme park industry and a use at last for all that awkward Christian heritage which has been such a burden to the Irish.

CELTWORLD: EVIL
EYES AND HISTORY

In 1949, Sean O'Faolain reported that an old West Cork woman had recently been been asked whether she believed in fairies. "I do not," she replied "but they're there." If that wonderfully perverse ambivalence about the Otherworld is no longer so marked a presence in our culture, the same spirit nevertheless persists in our wider sense of cultural identity. The mythological Ireland — the Celts, the Gaels, the sacred unity of the island — is something we no longer believe in. Yet we know it's there. And because we no longer believe in it, are no longer imprisoned by the myths, we can begin to take delight in it, to enjoy it as a form of entertaining fascination.

If you wanted to introduce someone to Ireland, the best place to start would be at the Celtworld "experience" in Tramore. It is a great introduction, not because the way to understand Ireland is to begin with the Celts or any such guff as Charles Haughey's stated belief that partition was "inconceivable" because of the "cultural unity" of ancient Ireland, but because the delightful mixture of high tech and low kitsch, of postmodern building and premodern fantasy, of seriousness and fantasy, of hippy mysticism and ancient piety, is a brilliant mirror of the state of the nation.

At first glance, the whole notion of Celtworld is absurd — a ridiculous clash between the prehistoric content (the Tuatha de Danaan, Cuchulain, Fionn Mac Cumhail and so on) and the futuristic medium (video, holograms, 3-D glasses, revolving seats, interactive displays). If the medium is the message, then the message is not, as the advertising for Celtworld claims: "a mytholgical experience which brings our past back to life," but the opposite: a glimpse of Ireland's future where we understand everything technologically and the mystical strain in our culture is finally assimilated to the norms of Hollywood fantasy.

Yet, to take such a view is to assume that there is something pure and uncorrupted in our Gaelic or Celtic past that is being contaminated. There isn't. Consider, for a moment, the source of most of the material used in the Celtworld displays. It is *The Book of Invasions*, compiled by monastic scribes in the 12th century. As recently as the last century, its narrative of the successive invasions of Ireland by Formorians and Milesians, Firbolgs and Tuatha de Danaan was considered to be genuinely historical. People of my generation still learned it in primary school as quasi-historical. But it was, of course, a highly imaginative and highly purposeful set of inventions. It bore about the same relationship to the actual world of pre-Christian Ireland as Celtworld does to the 12th century.

In a funny way, therefore, the creators of Celtworld have managed to do something analagous to what the 12th century scribes must have done with whatever material they were working with in creating their myths of Irish origins. This is true in two respects. In the first place, the inventors of *The Book of Invasions* set out, as Sean O'Faolain described it "to explain, with considerable imaginative power, how it was that a variety of people seemed to have settled, from time to time, in this now supposedly purely 'Gaelic' island." Today, too, if we have to have myths of origin, it is better to have multiple and complex ones, such as you get at Celtworld via *The Book of Invasions*, emphasising diversity, rather than simplistic myths of racial purity.

And secondly, before we complain that Celtworld is reductive — bringing the gods of the early invaders down to the level of Marvel comic heroes — it is well to remember that so were the compilers of *The Book of Invasions*. Their purpose was precisely to give a reduced human origin to the remaining pagan deities and demi-gods, to explain their traces in landscape and belief as memories of a defeated race of mortal invaders rather than as hidden and still-powerful supernatural forces. The brilliantly imaginative explanation of the fairies as descendants of the Tuatha de Danaan, driven underground after their defeat in the Battle of Moytura, is a sophisticated way of saying "They're there but I don't believe in them." Celtworld, therefore, is no more reductive than The Book of Invasions itself.

Indeed, it is in some respects considerably more expansive. What you get at Celtworld is a kind of palimpsest, a manuscript which has been written over but on which the original writing still comes through in discernible but undecipherable forms. Or rather a bizarre series of such over-written manuscripts. Behind it all is a pre-Christian mythology. Written over that is a 12th century re-invention of it, then a 19th century pre-Raphaelite visualisation of the mytholgical, then a 1960s hippy re-invention of the pre-Raphaelites (the graphics are by Jim Fitzpatrick, whose images of the Celtic world are inextricable from Flower Power) and finally 1990s technology. The result is not a vision of Ireland's legendary past, but a wonderfully accurate version of present-day Irishness, a bizarre accumulation of heterodox imaginings.

Making some kind of sense of it all is the feeling that technology is our Otherworld just as magic was the Otherworld of the Celts. One of the best of the special effects at Celtworld is Balor's Evil Eye, itself so reminiscent of a video screen or a modern weapon of war.

Indeed, if you read the description of the Evil Eye in *The Book of Invasions* it is hard not to be struck by how reminiscent it is of a machine: "An Evil Eye had Balor of the Formorians. That eye was never opened save on the battle-field. Four men used to lift up the lid of the eye with a polished handle which passed through its lid. If an army looked at the eye, though they were many thousands in number, they could not resist a few warriors..." If the army lying stunned before that machine-like eye reminds you of your kids watching television, you are well on the way to appreciating Celtworld.

GOING NATIVE

The Irish as Black as Indians

"It was terrible weather too," said the policeman, "the day a nun found the dead Redskin on Duke Street... No one ever found out where he came from, who he belonged to, no poison was found in him nor any sign of violence on him: he was clutching his tomahawk, he was in war paint and all his war finery, and since he had to have a name - we never found out what his real name was — we called him 'our dear red brother from the air'. 'He's an angel', wept the nun — she wouldn't leave his side — 'he must be an angel; just look at his face...'".
— Heinrich Boll, Irish Journal (1957)

In October 1992, in the grounds of the community centre in Killinkeere, County Cavan, near the Irish border, a tree was planted in a ceremony of reconciliation. It was not, as might be supposed, a gesture of reconciliation between Protestants and Catholics, but between the Irish and the Indians. Killinkeere is the reputed birthplace of General Philip Sheridan, the American general who coined the phrase "the only good Indian is a dead Indian." A plaque on a house up a quiet lane on the road to Bailieboro, placed there by the American army, records the origins of the great Indian killer. Up that road, after more than a century, came a Native American woman, Joanne Tall from South Dakota, with her daughter ReaAnn, Oglala Sioux and descendants of Chief Crazy Horse. She came to reconcile this strange fact of Irish history, to plant a weeping willow and to exorcise a painful past. It stands there now amidst the fields, small but growing, an odd, inscrutible symbol of an unfamiliar Ireland, an Ireland nevertheless that makes more sense in the 1990s than many other versions of the place.

"Your music," says Jimmy Rabbitte in the most popular Irish novel of recent years, Roddy Doyle's *The Commitments*, "should be about where you're from and the sort of people you come from." Nothing there, in essence, that could not have been said by Yeats or Synge or Lady Gregory, all of whom believed that a culture should be about the place and the people you come from. It's the bit that comes next that they might have had difficulty with: "'Say it once, say it loud, I'm black and I'm proud.' They looked at him.'James Brown...' They were stunned by what came next. 'The Irish are the niggers of Europe, lads.' They nearly gasped, it was so true. 'An' Dubliners are the niggers of Ireland ... An' the Northside Dubliners are the niggers of Dublin — Say it loud I'm black an' I'm proud.'"

How did we get from the beginning of that passage to the end, from Yeats to James Brown, from the idea of national cultural distinctiveness to the desire not just to be somebody else, but to be a different race, and an oppressed one at that? And why do you find, in works by younger Irish writers from urban communities, conscious usage of imagery linking the Irish not just to the blacks but to the Indians, a linkage that is sometimes playful and comic, but sometimes serious and almost literal.

Why is one of the finest recent Irish novels, *Black Robe*, by the Belfast novelist Brian Moore, about a French missionary travelling into the great Canadian forests in the 17th century to convert the Indians to Catholicism, a brilliant reversal of Irish colonial and religious history, in which the Irish both are and are not the Indians?

Why in Paul Muldoon's laconic poem *Meeting the British* is the encounter of Ireland and England sardonically encapsulated in the encounter of Indian and white man? Why is perhaps the most accomplished play by any of the younger generation of Irish playwrights, Sebastian Barry's *White Woman Street*, an epic of the Wild West in which the Irish hero is haunted by the death of a young prostitute who was sold as being white but was really an Indian? Why in one of the most powerful Irish theatrical events of the 1990s, Druid's production of Vincent Woods' *At the Black Pig's Dyke*, do Leitrim mummers appear at times as Indian war-dancers? Why is the first published story of one of the most accomplished young novelists, Joe O'Connor's *The Last of the Mohicans*, an ironic play on the romance of the Indians? Why, in other words, is one of the characteristics of the new urban literature emerging in Ireland a desire to play with being black or Indian? This is an odd question, and to attempt to answer it requires a long diversion into the place from which urbanised Ireland takes its shapes, America.

In his great history of the Indian Wars of the eighteenth century, *The Conspiracy of Pontiac* (published in 1851) the American historian Francis Parkman makes a curious, unexplained connection in which a Frenchman who intermarries with the Indians becomes an Irishman, or at least a Celt. With all the disdain of the Boston brahmin for the compromise between civilisation and barbarism, Parkman sketches out the nightmare of cultivated society going native, of the forest encroaching on the town:

"From the beginning, the French showed a tendency to amalgamate with the forest tribes...At first, great hopes were entertained that, by the mingling of French and Indians, the latter would be won over to civilisation and the church; but the effect was precisely the reverse; for, as Charlevoix observes, the savages did not become French, but the French became savages. Hundreds betook themselves to the forest, nevermore to return. These outflowings of French civilisation were merged in the waste of barbarism, as a river is lost in the sands of the desert. The wandering Frenchman chose a wife or a concubine among his Indian friends; and, in a few generations, scarcely a tribe of the west was free from an infusion of Celtic blood."

The use of the adjective "Celtic" in this vision of an Eden tarnished by original sin is strange but significant. The

French would not generally be regarded as Celts, and, given that Parkman's book was written in Boston at the height of "native" (i.e. WASP) American hysteria about the arrival of the Famine Irish, it is not hard to guess at the real source of his fear and disgust. The wild, ill-clad, superstitious savages, who might swamp civilisation with their barbarism, mixing native and Celtic blood, were heeling up every day in Boston harbour.

In the course of his epic history, Parkman makes the image of the Celt, and specifically the Irishman as the locus of impurity, the dread crossroads at which civilisation and barbarism meet, more explicit. He writes with some fascination of the figure of Sir William Johnston, "a young Irishman" who went to America in 1734 and gained a huge tract of land in New York. Johnston was the major-general who commanded the English forces against the French at the Battle of Lake George. He was also superintendent of Indian affairs. His mistress, known as Molly Brant, was the sister of the Iroquois war chief. As a letter of Johnston's from 1765 shows, he also dressed and behaved like an Indian, or, as he put it more delicately to the Board of Trade "I was called to the management of these people, as my situation, and opinion that it might become one day of service to the public, had induced me to cultivate a particular intimacy with these people, and even to their dress on many occasions."

When the American War of Independence was beginning to break out, Johnston, Irishman, subject of the English king, and brother to an Iroquois war chief, was faced with a terrible dilemma. If he remained loyal to the king, he would be required to lead his Indian army against his fellow American settlers. To be a proper white man, to prove his loyalty as the King's general, he would have to set the barbarians on the civilised people. In what Parkman calls an "agony of indecision," he went mad and died suddenly, reputedly by his own hand. At the birth of the modern world, a now forgotten Irishman was plunged, by the impossible ambivalences of Irishness, caught between barbarism and civilisation, into madness and death.

Johnston's death as the modern world was entering its most decisive act of emergence, the birth of America, had a history and a culture. For Puritan civilisation, the plantation of Ireland and the contemporaneous plantation of America were inextricable. Christopher Hill, Oliver Cromwell's biographer, tells us that "we should see Cromwell's Irish policy as part of his general imperial policy. The native Irish were treated much as the original settlers of New England treated the Indians. Cromwell wrote to New England to try to persuade 'godly people and ministers' to move to Ireland." Presumably their experience of civilising the Indians would come in handy with the Irish.

The Puritans had an ambivalence about plantation which derived from the fear of contamination and degeneracy. John Owen preached in 1685 that "we are like a plantation of men carried into a foreign country. In a short space they degenerate from the manners of the people from whence they came and fall into that of the country whereunto they are brought." The only plantation of which Owen had first-hand experience was Ireland, which is obviously the source of his image.

Frances Hutcheson in his *Inquiry into the Origin of our Ideas of Beauty and Virtue* (1725), itself a formative influence on the American revolution, remarks sardonically on "the horror and admiration of the wondrous barbarity of the Indians, in nations no stranger to the massacre at Paris, the Irish rebellion, or the journals of the Inquisition," a phrase in which the violence of Catholics against Protestants, among them the Irish Catholic rebels, is explicitly linked to that of the Indians.

In America, the link between the Irish massacres of Protestants and the massacre of Indians became explicit in a supremely ironic way. In 1764, when Irish

Presbyterians massacred the Contestoga Indians, they were accused of savagery by the Quakers of Philadelphia. A contemporary letter notes that "the Presbyterians, who are the most numerous, I imagine, of any denomination in the province, are enraged with their being charged in bulk with these facts, under the name of Scotch-Irish, and other ill-natured titles, and that the killing of the Contestoga Indians is compared to the Irish massacres, and reckoned the most barbarous of either."

The Quakers of Philadelphia gave the Indians shelter and the Irish backwoodsmen marched on the city, which had to be barricaded. For a brief moment, in the New World, the Irish were the Indians outside the walls of the civilised city. The Indians and the Quakers were the civilians inside. In this state, though they were Ulster Presbyterians, they could only be thought of by the defenders of Philadelphia as Irish Papists. A satiric poem circulated by the Quakers inside the city pictured the leader of the Presbyterian attackers as an archetypal Irish papist;

O'Hara mounted on his Steed,
Descendant of that self-same Ass,
(That bore his Grandsire Hudibras,)
And from that same exalted station,
Pronounced an hortory oration:
..."Dear Sirs, a while since
Ye know as how an Indian Rabble
With practices unwarrantable,
Did come upon our quiet Borders,
And there commit most desperate murders..."
He paused, as Orators are used,
And from his pocket quick produced
A friendly vase well stor'd and fill'd
With good old wiskey twice distill'd,
And having refreshed his inward man,

Went on with his harangue again.

The bluster, the whiskey, the absurd self-importance — all of the classic stereotypes of the Irishman are present, even in the view taken by one white Protestant of another. What matters is that the Irishman, in his slaughter of the Indians, has become himself a savage. He is, both literally and metaphorically, outside of the bounds of civilisation.

It is important to remember that this myth of the Celtic Indian was no mere momentary invention. It had roots that went back as far as the colonisation itself, though principally in a Welsh, rather than Irish, form. As early as the thirteenth century, stories of the discovery of magical islands to the west by a Welsh seafarer Madoc circulated in Europe. The Elizabethan polymath, Dr John Dee, transmuted these stories into a Welsh discovery of America as a weapon against Spanish claims on the New World. In the mid-18th century, this myth resurfaced as the early Welsh settlers in America began to report the existence of Welsh-speaking Indians, the descendants of Madoc. Scores of people reported conversations in Welsh with Indians. Several Indian chiefs swore to their Welsh ancestry. Many men told tales of having their lives saved by talking in Welsh to their Indian captors. At least 13 real tribes were identified as Madoc's descendants and a further eight invented for the purpose. By the end of the eighteenth century, Madoc fever was raging all over the USA and belief in these Celtic Indians was almost universal. Indeed, much of the most important early exploration of the western frontiers was carried out in search of Welsh Indians.

Out of this strange dialectic of civilisation and barbarism, came the possibility of real Celts identifying themselves as Indians. In 1800-1, a virtual civil war in parts of Maine was conducted between the landed proprietors, chiefly General Henry Knox, on the one hand, and the so-called White Indians on the other. The White Indians were the European poor who had settled in the forests, chief among them the Irish. These were the kind of backcountry squatters of whom A.J. Dallas, a New York landlords' lawyer complained in 1808 that "The Indians have hardly withdrawn from the ground and they are succeeded by a population almost as rude and as ferocious as themselves, coming for the most part from countries where the poor know nothing of the blessings of property and care little about its rights." Ireland, of course, was pre-eminent among such countries.

The Maine backwoodsmen were largely Ulster Irish living in the forests around the settlement of Belfast. In July 1800, General Knox's surveyors were ambushed by backwoodsmen "blacked and disguised like Indians" and three were wounded. A year later, with the skirmishes continuing in the meantime, the backwoodsmen marched on the settlement of Belfast, "dressed in Indian stile and perfectly black," making more explicit the dynamic of the march on Philadelphia in 1764: the White Indians outside the town, the civilised whites inside. Except that this time, the backwoodsmen were identifying themselves as Indians rather than setting out to slaughter Indians.

What we see in this shift is the emergence of the doubleness of the Celtic Irishman in racial imagery, the possibility that the identification with barbarism, black or Indian, can be a racial slur, or, alternatively, a badge of defiance. In the "scientific" discourse on race which dominated so much of post-Darwinist debate in Britain this doubleness is taken to the extreme of assuming that there were White Celts and Black Celts. The great Darwinian Thomas Huxley, even in defending the Irish against racial slurs, speculated on the existence of Black Celts:

"I am unaware of the existence of a dark-complexioned people speaking a Celtic dialect outside of Britannia (Ireland). But it is quite certain that in the time of Tacitus, the Silures, who inhabited South Wales and Shropshire, were a dark-complexioned people; and if Irish tradition is to be trusted for anything, we must credit its invariable assertion that only the chief Irish tribes — that of the Milesians — consisted of dark-haired, black-eyed people... In Ireland, as in Britain, the dark stock predominates in the west and south, the fair in the east and north... I believe it is this Iberian blood which is the source of the so-called black Celts in Ireland and in Britain."

Given that the Irish, racially, can be regarded as black or white or anything in between in the 19th century, it is not surprising that non-Irish writers kept up their casual identification of the Irish with the Indians, and that, sometimes, the Irish chose to turn this intended slur into a badge of pride.

We find, for instance, Parkman in 1851 describing the behaviour of Indian women in grief:

"All day they ran wailing through the camp; and when night came, the hills and woods resounded with their dreary lamentations... The outcries of the squaws on such occasions would put to shame an Irish death howl."

We find an English journalist in Tuam, Co Galway, in 1893 writing that, "not only are the cabins in this district aboriginal in build but they are also indescribably filthy and the condition of the inmates is no whit higher than that obtaining in the wigwams of the native Americans. The hooded women, black-haired and bare-footed, bronzed and tanned by constant exposure, are wonderfully like the squaws brought from the Far West by Buffalo Bill."

We find the *London Times*, after the great Irish famine of the 1840s remarking with some satisfaction that "an Irishman on the banks of the Shannon will soon be as rare as an Indian on the banks of the Manhattan."

But all of this imagery depends on its source, on the distinction between city and forest, on the fear of degeneracy which the intermixing of races would bring, on the contrast between civilisation and barbarism which the divide between town and forest or city and wilderness implies. What happens when there is no such distinction, when the Irish become urbanised? This happened in America long before it happened in Ireland, since the Irish in the nineteenth century urbanised themselves, not in Ireland, but in the great cities of America and Britain.

What happened is that the identification of Irish and Indian, set free of its moorings in fear of the forest, became playful, theatrical and a badge of pride. The same did not happen in relation to identification of Irish and blacks, because, after all, there were real blacks in New York and Chicago, and the Irish were often in direct competition with them. Two instances of this theatricalisation, the aestheticisation of the image of the Irish savage, can be mentioned. The first is in relation to Buffalo Bill Cody, whose Wild West Shows were the medium through which the Indians became a commodified image. Cody's Irish ancestry was probably fairly distant, but it is important enough in the making of his showbusiness legend to be placed, in a comically exaggerated form, at the very beginning of the 1899 official family biography of Buffalo Bill by his sister Helen Cody Wetmore:

"The following genealogical sketch was compiled in 1897. The crest is copied from John Rooney's *Genealogical History of Irish Families*. It is not generally known that genuine royal blood courses in Colonel Cody's veins. He is a lineal descendant of Milesius, King of Spain, that famous monarch whose three sons, Heber, Heremon and Ir, founded the first dynasty in Ireland, about the beginning of the Christian era. The Cody family comes through the line of Heremon. The original name was Tireach, which signifies 'The Rocks'. Muireadach Tireach, one of the first of the line, and son of Fiacha Straivetine, was crowned king of Ireland, Anno Domini 320. Another of the line became king of Connaught, Anno Domini 701. The possessions of the Sept were located in the present counties of Clare, Galway and Mayo. The names Connaught-Galway, after centuries, gradually contracted to Connallway, Connell-way, Connelly, Conly, Cory, Coddy, Coidy, and Cody, and is clearly shown by ancient indentures still traceable among existing records."

Note in particular how close the racial ideology is to that already referred to in Huxley's consideration of black and Iberian Celts. Note also that it is regarded as the essential beginning of the life of the man who was able to slaughter real Indians and then turn their image into a powerful international commodity.

The second aspect of this urbanised use of the identity of Irish and Indian is that most powerful Irish institution in the 19th and early 20th centuries, Tammany Hall in New York. Tammany Hall was the political institution through which the Irish controlled the politics of New York for decades. It was named after the 17th century chief of the Delaware Indians, and its twelve leaders were called Sachems (the Indian word for chiefs), headed by the Grand Sachem. On Tammany Day, May 12th, it held a parade with hundreds of "braves" marching through the streets with painted faces and carrying bows, arrows and tomahawks. When the Irish took over this institution, the White Indian had become not merely a gesture of backwoods protest, but a triumphant display of new urban power.

What was possible for the New York Irish at the turn of the century, however, was not possible for the Irish in Ireland at the same time, and did not become possible until they, too, began to develop a confidently urban self-image in the 1980s. In Ireland, at the turn of the century, the identification with blacks or Indians was still a real racial slur, still a tool of colonial oppression. The forest was real, not a literary metaphor. Rather than celebrate the White Indian or the Black Celt, they had to fend off the slur of racial impurity, of the notions of barbarism and degeneracy which went with it. The kind of Irishness which Buffalo Bill boasted about in his genealogy was impossible when Bufflo Bill's Wild West Show was being used, as in the report already quoted, as a horrible image of the inferiority of the Irish.

Instead, Irish literature set itself the task of inventing a counter-myth of national purity. Against the aestheticised celebration of impurity they set an insistence on the purity of the Gael, an image of the true Irish Gaelic peasant as the last remainder of an immemorial, untouched line. For the mainstream of Irish literature, the inherited categories were reversed. It was the city (ie England) which was degenerate, the wilderness which was pure. Parkman is turned on his head, but not in any way transcended. Canon Sheehan's novel *Luke Delmege* sums up the view of degeneracy when Fr Martin tells Luke: "I never think of England but as in that dream of Piranesi — vast Gothic halls, machinery, pulleys, and all moving with the mighty, rolling mechanism that is crushing into a dead monotony all the beauty and picturesqueness of the world." The countryside, meaning the Irish countryside, was the only true realm of authenticity and purity.

Yet this reversal was of no use to an emerging urban culture. Its need was not for an assertion of purity, which was anyway unsustainable in the context of a transatlantic culture as much influenced by Hollywood and the Rolling Stones as by the wood and stone of the Irish landscape, but for a way of celebrating impurity, of using the available aesthetic images of popular culture to speak about one's own society. For writers who grew up with Hollywood westerns and black-inspired rock and roll music, Indians and blacks were available images that had both the texture of contemporary pop culture and an ironic subconscious prehistory in the most useful aspects of the Irish past, the Irish past that happened in America.

The availability of these images to Irish writers now does not depend on an appreciation of the more obscure corners of early American history. The White Indian is available in films such as John Ford's *The Searchers*, which is at one level about Ireland and America, but also in films which have nothing to do with Ireland, such as Werner Herzog's *Fitzcarraldo*, where the hero, played by Klaus Kinski is an improbable Irishman, Brian Sweeny Fitzgerald, red hair and all, doing battle with the forest, in this case the Amazon rain forest. Somehow, when a dialectic of forest wilderness and urban civilisation is at stake, an Irishman is essential to the equation, even in a German film set in Amazonia. Think as well of Kipling's novel, *Kim*, where the mediation between India and imperial Britain, between wilderness and empire is carried on through the hero, an Irish boy named Kimball O'Hara. Or think in another context of Lawrence of Arabia, the most famous mediator between the Empire and the Arabs, and his fantasy that he was really the son of an Irishman, George Bernard Shaw.

In the emerging Ireland of the 1960s and after, the White Indian became a way of replacing history with irony, identity with a mongrel freedom, post-colonial angst with jokey doubleness. The new Tammany Hall politicians of 1960s Fianna Fáil — the up-coming generation of Charles Haughey, Brian Lenihan and Donough O'Malley — were dubbed "The Mohawks" by their sceptical colleague Kevin Boland. Their attitude to the letter of the law was also distinctly Wild West, encapsulated in O'Malley's story of being caught driving the wrong way up a one-way street and of his reply to the policeman who caught him: "See the arrows, guard? To tell the truth, guard, I didn't even see the bloody Indians."

As with the Irish who strutted down the streets of New York in Indian garb to proclaim their new-found power, to celebrate the fact that the savages had conquered civilisation, the Indian metaphor has been taken on by contemporary Irish culture as a device which frees it from the burden of identity and lets it loose to play games with the world.

In Paul Muldoon's poem, *The More a Man Has the More a Man Wants*, stray Indians stalk the nightmare of the Northern troubles, including

> *A Sioux. An ugly Sioux.*
> *He means, of course, an Oglala*
> *Sioux busily tracing the family tree*
> *of an Ulsterman who had some hand*
> *in the massacre at Wounded Knee.*

"Oglala" is a an echo of Gallogly, the poem's terrorist will-o'-the-wisp hero, and the identification frees the Northern conflict within the bounds of the poem from history, from place and from cliché. The Irish Indian allows for ironies and parodies, for free play within the prison of relentless fact. A similar effect is achieved in Muldoon's poem *Meeting the British*, in which the Irish are identified with the Indians in their approach to the arrival of British power.

Brian Moore's demolition of colonial angst in *Black Robe* goes even further, the tale of Catholic colonisation of the Indians of Canada carrying clear echoes of Ireland, but wrong-footing any simple post-colonial analysis by making the invader Catholic.

The re-invention of Irish history in Sebastian Barry's play, *White Woman Street* performs a similar function for the South, playing on the guilt of its central character, an Irish outlaw in the Wild West, in relation to his part in the destruction of the Indians. What is particularly striking in the play is that it turns on the doubleness of the dead woman, who is an Indian advertised as a white woman, an image that returns us directly to the origins of the metaphor with the White Indians in the early 19th century wilderness.

This tragic irony turns comic in Joe O'Connor's story, *Last of the Mohicans*, in which the title is a flip reference to the most famous literary image of the White Indian, giving a sly significance to the hero's floating existence in London and his mock-heroic stature as a rebel without a cause. Again, the Mohawk surfaces as a way of dealing with a new rootless urban generation that would otherwise be outside of the terms of any historical reference.

What contemporary Irish culture is doing in all of this is demolishing the colonial opposition of Self and Other and re-inventing the ideal of the Self as Other. It is bored with the old confrontations of England and Ireland, city and country, civilisation and barbarism, and prefers to play with the fruitful paradoxes which its peculiar history has made possible — the foreign native, the white black, the civilised barbarian. It is enjoying the benefits of a long history of being on the borders of two worlds and turning its dread status of being neither one thing nor the other into the playful pleasures of being both and neither. The lost tribe of Celtic Indians has found a home on the range.

SCARLETT FEVER

Phil Lynott thou shouldst be living at this hour. The man who invented the public persona of the black Irishman would have enjoyed two things which are happening in the world of popular culture. In the first place, up on the silver screens of cinemas around the world are the white Dublin boys of *The Commitments* proclaiming "I'm black and I'm proud." This is very funny, but much funnier is the sequel to *Gone With The Wind*, published in 1991.

In Alexandra Ripley's (the name is just too good to be true) *Scarlett* our feeble attempts to be black and proud are massively outdone by the ingenious device of transferring Scarlett's Tara back to the real Tara in County Meath, making the deep south of Ireland much deeper then we thought. The bulk of the novel is set not in Savannah, but in Ireland, with our goodselves, our puny little history and our stray fragments of a culture appropriated to the continuance of a quintessential American Story. And what is most hysterical is that the Irish act as a direct and almost explicit replacement for the black slaves of Tara.

You can see the problem which Ms. Ripley had to solve. Stories like that of *Gone With The Wind* conventionally happened to queens, princesses or at least duchesses. The genre is essentially that of the costume romance, which depends on having a few royals around. Unfortunately, beastly America doesn't offer any such comforts, hence the attraction of the southern plantation, which is a kind of self-governing country with its own king and queen and its own subjects. But if you're going to depend on the romance of the plantation, you have to hide the basis of its life: slavery. The black slaves have to be part of the family, their devotion freely given. Hence all those rolling eyes and quivering lips in *Gone With The Wind*.

Sadly, since the days of Margaret Mitchell, the blacks have got awkward. They resent the fact that their greatest acting talents were reduced to lovable stereotypes in *Gone With The Wind*. They are not going to take kindly to wide-eyed lines like "Why Miss Scarlett I don't know nothin' 'bout birth 'n' babies."

What is Ms. Ripley to do? She reaches into a dark and dusty attic called Ireland and out comes a jumble of faded hand-me-downs that can be refurbished for further use: faith-and-begorrah buckleppers, kindly priests, romantic Fenians, superstitious and garrulous peasants, and even an ancient round tower in which Scarlet and Rhett, when they get back together as they must in the end, can consummate their dark desires . You can have all the wild, picturesque and exotic charms of the darkies right here in our own little plantation.

With somewhat indecent haste Ms. Ripley kills off the lovable black Mammy and gets Scarlett to the Old Country as fast as her hobbled old nag of a plot will allow. Ireland, she is told, is where people "lived on their farms, in the countryside, with no city nearby at all, only a village with a church and a blacksmith and a public house where the mail-coach stopped. . . Travelling wagons came by with ribbons and trinkets and papers of pins." "But that's just like plantation life," Scarlett exclaimed.

For those of us who thought that Irish History was a complex affair, *Scarlett* comes as a great relief. Not only is Irish History all about the Irish killing the English, it is also all about the O'Haras killing the English. The O'Haras are the Fenians and always have been. Scarlett herself, since the Irish are very good at recognising the innate superiority of an American heroine, is quickly made The O'Hara of Ballyhara (you know the place, just left at Glacamarra and all the way home is down-hill). She rescues the peasants from their own indolence (much as the poor slaves needed the white man to show them how to work) and makes Ballyhara the centre of all Fenian activity. "You've done what's near miraculous, too, getting all these Irish to work the way they have. And spitting in the eyes of the English Officer."

It is, of course, the white woman's burden, a pale shadow of Kipling except that it is vastly less literate (Scarlett doesn't speak, she "verbalises") and in the service of the American empire, rather than the British. *In The White Man's Burden* Kipling sympathised with the Empire's burden of improving *"Your new-caught sullen peoples, Half-devil and half-child."*

Among the sullen peoples were, of course, the Irish and the Blacks. "The murders of this country," wrote a Victorian English traveller in Ireland, "would disgrace the most gloomy wilds of the most savage tribes that ever roamed in Asia, Africa or America." The child side of the tribes from the gloomy wilds is their innocence and their need to be mothered. The devil side is their sullen ingratitude, the possibility that at any moment they might go mad and murder the civilised people in their beds.

And, alas for poor Scarlett, the Irish are just like this. One minute she is The O'Hara performing all their rituals for them, including the well-known ceremony of Planting the First Potato, the next minute they are untamed animals howling for her blood. The village blacksmith who is such a picturesque part of the evocation of Ireland earlier in the book is out after her with his pike (every Irishman of course, keeps one in the thatch for the ceremony of Planting of the First Englishman). "Scarlett held her breath. The voices were so close, so inhuman, so like the yowling of wild beasts." Isn't that just typical of the Irish? You give them Mickey Mouse and MacDonald's and International Financial Services Centres and lots of green cards, and before you know it they're chasing you with their pikes.

On the credit side, it has to be said that Ms. Ripley has worked very hard to master Irish dialogue, history and folk customs. Not only has she uncovered the secrets of the

First Potato, she also knows that an Irish wake is punctuated with "why did you leave us? Ochon! Ochon, Ochon, Ullagon O," that an Irish story is typically about "the time Daniel and his brother Patrick, God rest his soul took the Englishman's prize pig and carried it down into the peat bog to farrow"; and that all civilised Irish people get *The Irish Times* every day and "everyone you will meet in Dublin will expect you to be familiar with the news it reports". This latter piece of accuracy stands out like a good deed in a naughty world.

In the end, it is nice to know that it has all been worth it, that all the massacres and famines and well-nursed wrongs of Irish history have at last found their fulfillment in Ms. Ripley's book. Was it not our own esteemed former Taoiseach, Charles Haughey who told the movie moguls at the Cork Film Festival in the early 1960s that if they were short of a few stories, we had plenty to offer? All that remains is for a formal pact to be concluded between ourselves and the Americans: they can have the Fenians, the Famine, the Wake and the Planting of the First Potato; we'll take *When a Man Loves a Woman*, *Sex Machine* and the joys of Soul. Looking at *The Commitments* and *Scarlett*, I think we'll get the best of the deal.

History

BORN AGAIN IN THE USA

For a very large proportion of the Irish people, and certainly for the way the rest of the world thinks about Ireland, the most important event of the week is not the atrocities in the North or Charles Haughey's gallstones or Paisley and the Pope or the problems of tax windfalls. It is the release of a new album by U2, *Rattle and Hum*, accompanied by a book and a film. We may not like the fact, but *Rattle and Hum* will have a more powerful shaping influence on the consciousness of Irish People under 25 than the *1916 Proclamation* or the *Nicean Creed*. We may be uncomfortable about it, but the album and the film will form the image of Ireland in America, Britain, Australia, Japan and the rest of the world more effectively than Noraid, the IDA, Bord Fáilte and Terry Wogan put together. It's about time, then, that aside from saying how wonderful Bono and the boys are, and how proud we all are of their achievements, we started to look at what it is they are saying, at what they are saying to us and about us.

It's true, of course, that U2 have become the most famous Irishmen of all time for relatively simple reasons. They write memorable songs, they have created an original sound in a medium desperately short of originality, they have the power to excite audiences in their live shows, and they are brilliantly marketed. But in their case, there is more to it than that. Their audiences don't just talk about being entertained, they talk about being inspired and uplifted. When *"Entertainment USA"* wants to define them, it doesn't talk about Bono's voice or the Edge's guitar style, it talks about social conscience and idealism. Political and spiritual values are an implicit part of U2, both for the image makers and the audience. Both Charles Haughey and Garret Fitzgerald in his time recognised this — it's no accident that U2 are invoked in party political broadcasts and Ard Fheis speeches, that mention of the band is the modern political equivalent of the rub of a relic. No accident either that the band's fanzine is called Propaganda.

So what is it that U2 are saying? The answer is not an easy one. The songs on *Rattle and Hum* invoke everyone from Charles Manson (*Helter Skelter*) to Martin Luther King (*Pride*). The words of Sunday Bloody Sunday look for a Christian forgiveness and renewal, the music, all military drum tatoos and machine-gun guitars, has the opposite effect. They talk of pacifism and wave tricolours. They talk of the fear of the nuclear apocalypse and yet their whole style is apocalyptic and messianic. They are against Apartheid, repressive regimes and Reaganite policies in Central America. Like all really successful icons of modern mass culture, they embody and incorporate many opposites, many contradictions. But in rock music, if there's a contradiction between words and images, between what is said and the way of saying it, then the image wins. Bruce Springsteen's *Born in the USA* may be an expression of blue collar anger at the establishment, but the four words of the title and the macho strut of the music were enough for Ronald Reagan to want to use it as the theme song for his 1984 re-election campaign.

What worries me about U2 is the image they have created and the images that they use. Their appeal in Ireland is essentially the same as their appeal in America — they have re-mythologised America, given new life to new images of America that no one other than Reagan has dared to tap in modern times. The band's official image, in their stage costumes, in the work of their photographer Anton Corbijn, in the video *Under a Blood Red Sky*, in the new movie of *Rattle and Hum*, draws on all the myths of the Wild West that even Hollywood has stopped using. Bono and The Edge wear cowboy hats, bandanas, lariats, cowboy boots. Corbijn photographs them in the Arizona desert or against the tumble down Wild West ghost-towns that none of us have seen since the shoot-out at the OK Corall. *Under a Blood Red Sky* has the band playing on the Colorado boulders that Indians used to appear behind. Adam Clayton, the band's bassist, says that the Arizona desert was "immensely inspirational" for their classic album *The Joshua Tree*. Bono says that "America both fascinates and frightens me, I can't get it out of my system." U2 have recreated a mythic America in a way that is enormously appealing to their largely white, middle-class American audience, and, I believe, enormously destructive for the Irish young.

It's no accident that the last person to use this Wild West landscape so successfully in invoking an archetypal, mythic America was another Irishman John Ford, in films like *Stagecoach* and *The Man Who Shot Liberty Valance*. We in Ireland have a terrible need to see America not just as a real place, but as an ideal, as something to believe in, something to escape to. The myth of America as a saviour and a refuge is something that has paralysed us for a very long time, keeping us from taking our own lives into our own hands. And this need for a mythic America has never been greater than it is now, never more powerful in its ability to convince young Irish people that life even as an illegal burger flipper in the Bronx is preferable to staying in Ireland and trying to change it.

What I don't like about U2 is that for all their obvious talent and patent decency, for all that they have given us images of success instead of the sordid satisfactions of glorious failure, they have revitalised something that for us, and I suspect for young Americans, would be better dead. Their combination of Wild West heroism and messianic posturing with the hard brash sound of rock and roll has been hugely effective in giving old myths new forms. In his darker moments, Ronald Reagan showed signs of seeing the nuclear apocalypse as a welcome return to the values of the Wild West, a universal desert populated by rugged idealists. U2's apocalyptic romanticism has used exactly the same imagery, informed by something of the same Christian fundamentalism. What's bad for us in U2's imagery is, in a different way, also bad for America. "How long?" as Bono asks in *Sunday Bloody Sunday* "How long must we sing this song?"

Irish Times, October 1988.

AN UNPREDICTABLE PAST

The inquest on Thomas Kirby was finally held in February, 1991. Held in Cashel, County Tipperary, it had all the usual trappings of such grim affairs: the coroner, the evidence of the State pathologist John Harbison, the account by the Garda superintendent of how he found the body. Yet the clues in this case had come not from police work or from sensational events, but from the work of Michael and Kitty Barry of the Clounalty Historical Society. History was at work.

The most important deposition at the inquest came from a 90-year old man, Michael O'Brien. He recalled the death of another local man, Thomas Kirby of Bansha. Kirby had joined the Lincolnshire regiment of the British Army in 1920 and deserted in 1921. He was then 36. Michael O'Brien remembered seeing Kirby around the place in the early months of 1921 and telling him that he was stupid to be seen around in his British uniform. Later, when Kirby was seen around no more, he heard talk that he had been shot by the IRA as a "spy".

In September 1990, Superintendent Peter Griffin and Dr John Harbison went to the State forest in Rossmore. They had been given a good idea where to look. They had the shallow grave carefully uncovered, and there was the body of a man in the uniform of the Lincolnshire Regiment. Because the soil was so boggy, it looked like the body of a man who had been recently buried. They took it out and Dr Harbison performed an autopsy. He confirmed that the man had been shot. From the trajectory of the bullets, he could tell that he had been shot while stooping, probably digging his own grave.

The haunting thing about the exhumation of Thomas Kirby was that it was both history and current affairs, both past and present. His murder could have happened in 1971 or 1991 as well as 1921, albeit in Northern Ireland rather than the Republic. It evoked a sense of the instability of history, of the way in which, in Ireland, history itself gives underfoot and forms no stable basis for the present. In many repects, the past is as open as the present.

Three years later, in Dublin, more bodies started to come up from the soil. The Sisters of Our Lady of Charity sold the cemetery of the Magdalen Home in High Park, Drumcondra, to property developers for over £1 million. A firm of undertakers, Patrick Massey Limited, was brought in to exhume the bodies of 133 forgotten women who had been incarcerated in the Home because they were judged to be "fallen," or in moral danger or merely homeless. They had worked in the Home's laundry, in many cases for most of their lives, forgotten, invisible, shut away. Now, even their resting place was not their own and they had to make way for the new economy. The first body had been buried there in 1866, the last in 1985. Over two weeks, they were disinterred, taken to Glasnevin cemetery, cremated and their ashes were buried in a mass grave.

One of the strange things about Ireland's relationship to history is that everything seems to be connected. You flip over a story about a high-tech global economy and you find yourself in the nineteenth century. You scratch polished surfaces and they bleed. In the same week as the story of the Magdalens was making the papers, the other big story, though it seemed to come from a differnt universe, had this kind of strange underground connection to it. It is a link that may not in itself be very important but that says much about the nature of history for us, the way the past keeps surfacing with a frantic gulp for air, before it disappears again beneath the waves.

The other big story was the replacement of Tony Ryan as chairman of Guinness Peat Aviation. It was the end of a piece of modern Irish history that lasted for barely a decade, an attempt to build a global aircraft leasing corporation in Ireland. It was a story from a world where things do not last, where empires rise and fall in the blinking of a historical eye. It was the kind of story that implies that, in the global economy, history really is bunk.

The Magdalen story, though, like that of Thomas Kirby, was a story of history literally disinterred. A few days before it broke, the historian Dr Mary Cullen was telling the Desmond Greaves summer school that women were beginning to rediscover their history, their "lost group memory". While she spoke, though, the graves of the Magdalen women in the High Park convent in Drumcondra, Dublin, were being emptied and the remains of those who lay there cremated and shifted to the mass graves in Glasnevin. It was a haunting image of a history that remains largely unwritten, a history that in being disturbed still has the power to disturb.

What possible connection can there be between these two histories, between the fall of GPA and the digging up of graves in Drumcondra? The answer can be found on the GPA share register, itself a record of broken dreams. There with the banks and the businessmen, with the great and the good, is listed "Sr Kathleen Hanly, Convent of Our Lady of Charity, High Park, Drumcondra, Dublin, (joint account holders). 5,200 shares." This is the same convent that was disinterring the graves of 133 fallen and forgotten women. According to the Catholic Press and Information Office, the convent was short of money and needed to raise cash for further development at the convent.

At least part of its need for cash must have something to do with losses on GPA shares. The shares it held were purchased in 1991, when the price was very high. They cost about US$110,000 and became, when the company collapsed, all but worthless. That is a very substantial loss for a charitable institution to take.

There is about our relationship to history in Ireland a kind of equivalent to the uncertainty principle in physics, a sense that we cannot look simultaneously at the present and the past without disturbing the past itself. The image of the Magdalen women being unable to rest in peace in the Ireland of global capital, stock markets and business heroes we are trying to construct is, or at least should be, a haunting one. The past is full of unfinished business. It will not be finished until it is acknowledged and given its due.

One of the worst things about what the nuns at High Park did is that, however unintentionally, it repeated the original insult which society offered to the women in that asylum and others like it. At least 23 such homes for "fallen women" were established in the nineteenth century, but High Park is important because it was the largest such asylum in Ireland or England. For that reason alone it is exemplary, an embodiment of an underground history that is still largely unacknowledged. Historians like Catriona Clear and Maria Luddy, and the playwright Patricia Burke Brogan in her fine play *Eclipsed*, have tried to rescue the Magdalen homes from amnesia. But it is significant that the last line of Maria Luddy's essay on the subject in *Women Surviving* is that "these women, perhaps the most hidden group in Irish society, do have a history which deserves to be recorded." While that work of rescuing a memory was being contemplated, the most basic memorial, the graveyard, was being obliterated.

The repeated insult is precisely that, in life, these women who are part of a forgotten past were told again and again to forget the past. High Park's own report for 1881 stressed that "Until the penitents forget the past, nothing solid can be done towards their permanent conversion." The women, ex-prostitutes, women who had children out of wedlock, orphaned girls, or even "women perceived to be in danger of losing their virginity," were forcibly cut off from their own histories. Their children, if they had them, were taken from them, they were not allowed to write or receive letters, and they were hardly ever allowed vistors. The past was the enemy to be defeated, personal history a history of shame.

There is, of course, nothing that Irish society now can do for those dead women. Except, that is, let them rest in peace. For our own sakes, though, we need to remember and understand the history of such women and such institutions. It is a history of what happens when a society chooses not to take responsibility for its own problems and to confine them, under a cloak of religiosity, to some place out of sight and out of mind. The history of the Magdalen homes, of the borstal homes run by orders of brothers, of the orphanages and asylums, is a history of a chosen forgetfulness. In other forms, that forgetfulness is still a constant danger. Forgetting the past helps us to forget the present, to keep out of mind today's outcasts and aliens. To compound that forgetfulness, to give that shameful history the sanction of the present, is both dangerous and disgraceful.

This is not just a problem for the nuns at High Park or even for the Catholic Church as a whole. These were Catholic institutions and the church did create and sustain many of the social attitudes which made these women outcast in the first place. But they had as much to do with Victorian England as with Rome, with the pathological connection between sexuality and madness which created the category of "moral insanity" into which such women were pushed. Many of the institutions existed before the nuns took them over, and the nuns probably ran them with more efficiency and, sometimes at least, charity than lay people had done. And it was, after all, respectable society which literally sent its dirty linen to be washed by the Magdalens.

THE MISSING CHANGE
THAT BINDS US

I met a man in 1990 from what was then still the Soviet Union. At the time, new revelations about his country's recent history were emerging every day, as the old archives were opened and new testimonies were allowed to be heard for the first time. What Stalin did, what Brezhnev, where the bodies were buried — these sorts of things were becoming known, for the first time. It struck me that it must be very strange to live in a country where what ought to be news — the day-to-day descriptions of events as they were happening — has to await history, and where conversely, history is news.

Last week, sitting in a room in Dublin Castle, where an inquiry into events now passed, an inquiry described by one lawyer as "industrial archaeology", was in progress and waiting to hear the latest news about events that happened between Charles Haughey and Sean Doherty in 1982 and ought to be history by now, I didn't have to wonder anymore. As in the Brian Lenihan tapes affair, the material of academic historical research on the one hand and the material of the latest sensational news on the other, had become indistinguishable. I remembered a phrase the Russian man had used: "These days, we say we live in a country with an unpredictable past." So, these days, do we.

It is easy to understand the frustration and despair of someone who lives from hand to mouth and from week to week at the way a country which refuses to see unemployment as a crisis can see events of 1982 as one. Yet these two things — economic failure and our obsession with the past — might be more closely related than they seem to be.

84

A boomerang thrown 10 years before whirled back into view and hit the Taoiseach, Charles Haughey, hard on the back of the neck. Apperently out of the blue, Sean Doherty claimed that he had given the transcripts on illegal phonetaps to Haughey in 1982. Haughey himself may prefer to think that he was smitten by the jawbone of an ass, but whatever metaphors you prefer, there is still something strange about a society where events long since buried can still effect such powerful consequences at the highest levels of power. The phone-tapping was not, after all, revealed for the first time last week, nor even did any clear new version of those events emerge. If you compare the power of the past felt here last week with the way such things are dealt with on our neighbouring island, you get some sense of how particular our way of dealing, or not dealing, with such things is.

For all the gleeful gloating of the British media in the last week about the weird and wonderful ways of the exotic Irish, lies and the abuse of power are not exactly unknown in modern British politics. In the same year as our phone-tapping scandal began, 1982, for instance, the British government set in train a much more serious sequence of evasions, half-truths and downright lies in relation to the sinking of the Argentine cruiser *General Belgrano*. The abuse of power was much more serious, involving as it did the loss of 368 lives rather than the abuse of the constitutional rights of three people. Furthermore, the truth of the affair became known much more quickly and much more fully. It did some damage to Mrs. Thatcher at the time. Yet, once it was over, it was over. It is unthinkable that had further revelations emerged while she was still in power she would have been forced to resign.

Why then does the past have such powerful and such devasting consequences in Irish politics? Why does it now seem that long-forgotton events, about which the evidence is contradictory rather than conclusive in both cases, will have brought down in little over a year first a Tanaiste, than a Taoiseach? How is it that we are so good at holding politicians responsible for the past when we are so bad at holding them responsible for the present; unemployment, emigration, and so on? To explain the huge contrast between the Irish and the English attitudes to scandals, a good place to start is with the historian Oliver MacDonagh in his superb book *States of Mind* : "In terms of norms and masses, it is true that the Irish do not forget and the English do not remember."

MacDonagh's analysis of the different conceptions of the past and its relationship to the present that obtain in Irish and in English culture is important because it suggests that, far from being a distraction for the task of solving present problems like unemployment, our obsession with the past may well be both a cause and a consequence of our failure in that task. We are obsessed with past events because we have little faith in our ability to change the present or the future. The past won't go away because the present is too much like it, too much burdened by the same problems. In this sense Mr. Haughey is the architect of his own downfall: his failure to move the country much beyond 1982 in social and economic terms, means that the past is still very much alive. The past is not another country, but the same old failed political entity it was 10 years ago.

Oliver MacDonagh suggests that two quite different notions of the past came to dominate thinking in Ireland and England. In Ireland, we came to think of the past as contemporaneous, as a moral court in which "no statute of limitations softens the judgement to be made on past events, however distant." Before making the words "time-frame" current Irish political usage, Mr. Haughey would have done well to read Professor MacDonagh: "The characteristic Irish time-frame inclines Irishmen to a repetitive view of history and such a view inclines them — perhaps in defensive wariness and in fear of failure — to prize the moral as against the actual, and the bearing of witness as against success." This could be an exact description of current events: a people steeped in failure and inured to the impossibility of change exulting in the moral pleasures of the just retribution against a sinner. By contrast, MacDonagh's analysis of the English attitude to the past as characterised by a linear view of progress in which everything supposedly moves forward with "a corresponding diminution of any sense of responsibility for the past" does much to explain the English facility for forgetting scandals like the Belgrano affair or Westland.

There may be a lot more moral satisfaction in our love of retribution than in their tendency to amnesia, yet it is hard not to believe that they get the best of the bargain. Leaving aside the dramatic and moral satisfactions of Mr. Haughey's come-uppance, what it reinforces above all is our awful fatalism and resigned disbelief in change. Since we don't believe that things change, we don't see why people shouldn't be held responsible to the fullest degree for what happened in the past. Incapable of giving us reasons to believe that we are not imprisoned by our past, our leaders have no right to complain when they are imprisoned by theirs.

Because of this, I can muster little sympathy for Charles Haughey. He has had more opportunity than anyone else in modern Ireland to show us that people and societies do change radically for the better and need not therefore be held responsible for what happened 10 or 20 years ago. He could have taught us to believe that history is a progress towards something better and not an endless re-run of old tragedies as new farces. Only in shifting us out of our past could he have made his own past irrelevant. He didn't and it isn't. Instead, he can only reflect like Shakespeare's Falstaff: "I have wasted time, and now doth waste me."

THE FACTS OF HISTORY

Citizen Robespierre, wrapped in the toga of a Roman emperor, is sitting in the studio of the great portrait painter of the Revolution, David. He is posing for posterity, frozen in the image he has chosen for history. He notices a giant canvas, on which David has begun his famous painting of the *Tennis Court Oath of June 20th, 1789*, the point of origin of the Revolution itself, the transforming moment from which Robespierre and all the revolutionary leaders draw their aura and authority. Amongst the patriots in epic poses he notices the freshly-painted head of Fabré d'Eglatine, who, at that very moment is on trial as a political enemy of Robespierre. He turns to David and orders "Wipe it out." "But," stumbles David, "he was there." His protest, however, is useless — the head of the "traitor" is obliterated from the painting, just as it will soon be struck off in reality. The great distortion of history has begun.

This is a scene, not from history, but from a film — *Danton* by the great Polish director, Andrej Wajda. It was made in 1983 as a Franco-Polish co-production, partly funded by the leftist French government as a lead-up to the celebrations of the 200th anniversary of the French Revolution, but made in the midst of the struggle in Poland between Solidarity and the Communists. This scene, therefore, was about French history, but it was also about contemporary Poland. The reference to the Stalinist practice of literally painting-out former heroes who had fallen from favour was not very oblique. It makes for a good scene and a good political message.

The only problem is that it could never have happened. Fabré d'Eglantine didn't take part in the Tennis Court Oath because he wasn't a deputy to the Estates General where it was sworn in monumental defiance of the king. So Wajda's fable about the distortion of history for the purposes of contemporary politics is itself a distortion of history for the purposes of contemporary politics. In order to expose the process of lying about history, the director, an artist of great courage and integrity, has had to lie about history. He made a film that was true to Poland, but so untrue to France that François Mitterand, after a private showing, started an anguished national debate about the teaching of history.

There is, in other words, no privileged point outside of history from which we can look dispassionately at the "facts" about the past and make firm judgements about its use or abuse. Everything we say about the past we say in the present, and the present is always full of its own concerns, its own meanings. With Jim Sheridan's film *In the Name of the Father* taking 7 Oscar nominations amid continuing attacks on its accuracy, its truth to the story of the Guildford Four and the Maguire Seven, it is worth recalling the paradox of Wajda's scene about history and falsification.

These are not small issues for film buffs to argue over. If you read, for instance, the reports of the funeral of the Republican terrorist Dominic McGlinchey , you cannot but be struck by the bitter conflict over the very identity of this man. Was he a vicious psychopath on the make, as most reports say, or an unsullied self-sacrificing Irish martyr, a latter-day Robert Emmet, as Bernadette McAliskey's funeral oration would have it? And how can two such fiercely opposed interpretations of the recent past co-exist?

The debate about *In the Name of the Father* is not all that new in the history of Irish politics. The first person to bring cinematic images to Connemara was Patrick Pearse, who brought a cinematograph operator down from Dublin to the school in Rosmuc, only to have the screening disrupted by an old woman who insisted on seeing "the real people" behind the screen. The most famous "documentary" images of the dying civilisation of the Aran Islands, the brilliant drama of the shark hunt in Robert

Flaherty's *Man of Aran* are an invention — the islanders hadn't hunted sharks for decades and had to be taught how to do so by experts brought in by the film-makers. Even while the myth of the lost Gaelic culture was at its most powerful as a political force, it was itself steeped in cinema. The past is sometimes most powerful when it is unreal.

If, however, such contradictions incline you towards scepticism about history itself, towards a belief that what happened in the past is merely a matter of choice and taste, then it is well to reflect that Europe just now may be suspended over the abyss by a thin sliver of memory. In the Europe of Zhirinovski, the Europe of ethnic cleansing, the Europe of Le Pen, the Europe of Italian media moguls flirting with fascism, the Europe of the casual abuse of foreigners by a Tory minister like Michael Portillo, only the memory of the Holocaust stands between us and potential chaos. We are stuck between a desperate need for the facts of history, and a growing awareness that the facts alone are insufficient and that their meaning will always be a matter of who we are and where we stand.

The dilemma is not just that the facts of history are shaped by the needs of the present. It is that a concern with the accuracy of the facts of history is itself a statement about the present. In a society where the present is relatively stable and uncomplicated, the facts of the past are important, but not a matter to get passionate about. In a society where the present reality is one of instability, division and danger, the facts about the past become critical.

When Poland was under Communist rule, for example, memorial plaques to Polish officers killed in the Katyn Forest massacre would often carry a single word — "1940". The date was of enormous significance, because if it were the proper date of death, then the massacre happened in 1940 and was perpetrated by the Russians, and not, as in the official version, in 1941, perpetrated by the Germans. Such plaques, therefore, became political statements.

Good, old-fashioned history of dates and events carried explosive meanings for the present.

In this sense, the debate about *In the Name of the Father* is not so much a contest between facts and artistic licence as one between a society that is sufficiently confident to search for meanings rather than facts, and one which is not. It is a contest between the Ireland of the Republic, delighted at taking its place among the Oscar-winning nations of the earth, and the embattled Ireland of the North, unable, it believes, to afford such luxuries.

And yet is not the challenge for the North precisely this need to take facts and make them into meanings? The North is weighed down by the tyranny of facts and dates: 1690, 1916, 1922, 1968, Bloody Sunday, Bloody Friday, bloody day after bloody day. Frizell's fish shop is a fact. So is the Greysteel Massacre. So is the hideous injustice of the Guildford Four. To take such facts and, without ever obliterating them, make them into fables, into stories, as Jim Sheridan has done, is not an ignoble thing. It is, on the contrary, a necessity, an essential part of the whole idea of peace. Stories have a beginning, a middle, and an end. Facts like the ones the people of the North have had to live with for 25 years, have a beginning and a middle. The ending has to be supplied by the imagination.

Irish Times, February, 1994

THE GHOST AND THE MACHINE

The legacy of the Kennedys

1.

After the torch had been passed to a new generation, after
his son had been sworn in as the 35th President of the
United States, old Joe Kennedy went to the celebration
lunch for his family which he had arranged at the
Mayflower Hotel in Washington. He found a huge table in
the buffet room, and hundreds of people milling around it.
He had never seen most of them in his life before, and he
was mightily annoyed. "Who are these people?" he asked
the social secretary who had organised the lunch. "Your
family, Mr Ambassador," she replied. "They are not. Just
who are these freeloaders?" Old Joe grabbed the nearest
half dozen guests and demanded to know their names.
Sure enough, they were Kennedys and Kennedy in-laws,
Bouviers and Fitzgeralds. "They are all family," Old Joe
admitted, "and it's the last time we get them all together
too, if I have anything to say about it." Meanwhile, down
on the old stone quay in New Ross, they were lighting
bonfires and brushing up on family connections.

When John F. Kennedy arrived at Dublin Airport thirty
years ago, he conjured up an image of a broken and
scattered family being re-united. He stood on the tarmac,
tanned and gleaming, and told us that "No country in the
world, in the history of the world, has endured the
haemorrhage which this island endured over a period of a
few years, for so many of its sons and daughters. These
sons and daughters are scattered throughout the world,
and they give this small island a family of millions upon
millions who are scattered all over the globe." In his words,
in his presence, was the tacit promise that all of these sons

92

and daughters and in-laws would be brought together again at the great buffet table of the post-war boom. But, in our hearts, we probably knew that when we arrived for the feast, we would still be confronted by a sour old man muttering "just who are these freeloaders?" and asked our names.

In retrospect, the ambivalence of that moment of arrival is striking. Even the image of family that was trotted out with such apparent comfort is disturbingly paradoxical. Eamon de Valera, President of Ireland, went to greet Kennedy at the airport and it was as if, here as well as in Washington, the torch was being passed to a new generation. There was a ceremonial, even ritual, air to the occasion, to this strange squaring of the circle. An Irish President born in Brooklyn came to do homage to an American President "from" New Ross. And to this strange symmetry was added the aura of a ritual succession of kingship, for these two men could have been father and son, and we were swopping the monkish, puritanical image of Ireland which de Valera embodied for the smooth, sexy, urbane Kennedy.

The disturbing question, though, was who was the father and who the son? President de Valera spoke to President Kennedy now as a proud father, now as a humble and grateful child. In his address of welcome, he spoke to Kennedy like a beaming Daddy who has called his boy into the study to congratulate him on his exam results. He called him "a distinguished son of our race" and told him frankly, "We are proud of you, Mr President."

But at other times, he spoke like an awed child, or like the chief of a remote tribe who has just been presented with a looking-glass and a necklace of cheap beads by a captain of the Royal Navy who is all the while eyeing his island for signs of removable wealth. He greeted Kennedy, not as President of America, but as "the first citizen of the great republic of the West, upon whose enlightened, wise and firm leadership hangs the hope of the world." The great republic of the West — the great white kingdom beyond the sea whose leader offers the natives fatherly protection and in return asks only for breadfruit. Had it been *Mutiny on the Bounty,* Kennedy would then have been offered a war dance and a choice of the young girls.

This ambivalence, this strange mixture of homage and absurdity, continued whenever Kennedy mentioned de Valera. In his address to the Oireachtas, for instance, he said that, "If this nation had achieved its present political and economic stature a century ago, my great-grandfather might never have left New Ross, and I might, if fortunate, have been sitting down there among you. Of course, if your own President had never left Brooklyn, he might be standing up here instead of me."

The words were ingratiating, and were obviously meant courteously, but the images they conjure up must, even then, have been comic and mocking: John F. Kennedy, parliamentary secretary to the Minister for Local Government answering questions about the state of the road between Ballina and Belmullet. Eamon de Valera and his lovely wife Jackie and their children Mick, Tadhg, Carmel and Concepta, having a quiet evening at the White House with their friends Marilyn Monroe and Frank Sinatra. It was a very big "if," so big as to remind us all the more forcefully of our dowdy little place in the world.

The same "if" was on Kennedy's lips when he spoke on New Ross quay about his great-grandfather: "If he hadn't left, I'd be working over at the Albatross Company, or maybe for John V. Kelly." The double-edge was cutting. On the one hand, every factory worker in New Ross could imagine himself, for an instant, as this tanned gorgeous man, radiating power and sex, and the thought, however instantaneous, could not be anything but pleasant. On the other hand, the instant after, the meaning of that sentence would clarify itself in the mind: "If we Kennedys hadn't got the hell out of here, even I'd be a no-good schmuck like you." Which would you rather be, the most powerful man in the world, or a member of John V. Kelly's loyal staff?

He went on, standing there on that quay, to tell a joke. It was the story of the New Ross man who emigrated to the States. He was doing alright, but not as well as emigrés have to pretend to be doing to the folks back home. So he went on a trip to Washington, and stood in front of the White House, and got a passer-by to take a picture of him. He sent the photograph back home, and written on the back were the words: "This is our summer house. Come and see it."

Did he know what he was doing, telling this story to us? Did he know that that was what all those photographs of his visit would be, a message to ourselves back home in our dreary lives, to pretend to ourselves that we were doing well? Did he know that the unwritten words on the backs of those photographs of our faces in the crowds, beaming at him in beatific bliss, pressing towards him as towards a messiah, were "This is my cousin. He came to see me"? Was he savouring the secret triumph of his power, that he was inside the White House, while we, poor Paddys, were standing outside the railings concocting false images to hide our failures?

He was a good actor, a star performer. He knew tricks that we were too naïve, too excited, too grateful, to see through. There was one particular trick that he used again and again on his visit here, and that we fell for every time, like the suckers we so badly wanted to be. He did it first in Cork, while he was accepting the freedom of the city. He stopped in the middle of his speech, looked out into the crowd, and said "I would like to ask how many people here have relatives in the United States. Perhaps they could hold up their hands?" And a forest of hands arose on the spot, hands reaching out towards him, waving towards him, wanting to be seen by him. Whether you had a relative in the States or not, you put up your hand, for how else could you identify yourself to him? And he smiled, and said "Well, I want to tell you they're doing well."

He did it again in Galway, and it worked again. And he did it again in Limerick, before he left. "I wonder before I go, if I could find out how many citizens here have relations in the United States, do you think you could hold up your hands if you do?" Again the hands went up, again we claimed the honour of having scattered our families. And again we were rewarded with a smile: "No wonder there's so many of them over there."

For decades those people in those crowds had listened to politicians and churchmen talking about the disgrace, the shame, the scandal of emigration. Yet here, on the streets of our cities, at the prompting of a showman's trick, we were holding up our hands to claim it, to wave it before the world. So desperate were we to respond to the first citizen of the great republic of the West that we could not be restrained from claiming our own disgrace. And in that, perhaps, for all the sham and neurosis of the event, there was some kind of healthy acknowledgement, some kind of truth. In the unseemly rush to claim Kennedy, we also had to claim all those other scattered families of ours, inglorious and unglamorous as they were. Those arms that reached out to him also had to grasp a painful history.

And, performer though he was, there is no reason to think that he was not also sincere in ways, that he was not also looking for something from us. Our hunger for his glamour, for his success, for his ease with the world and the flesh, was open, palpable, sometimes, as when the "cream" of Irish society made a show of itself by mobbing him at a garden party in the grounds of Áras an Uachtarain, pathetic. But he too may have had both personal and political desires which only we could fulfil.

At a political level, the agenda of his speeches was so clear that only our euphoria could stop it from being heard. He harped continually on the war against Communism, on the "most difficult and dangerous struggle in the history of the world," and there was nothing secretive about his desire for Ireland to play its part in that struggle by joining NATO. Even the sentimental versions of Irish history which he repeated were carefully pointed in this direction: "So Ireland is still old Ireland, but it has found a new mission in the 1960s, and that is to lead the free world, to join with other countries in the free world, to do in the 1960s what Ireland did in the early part of that century."

But even in this there was an unmistakable sense of a man trying to convince himself, as well as his listeners, of something. By the time he came here, Kennedy had already committed over 12,000 American "advisors" to Vietnam, and he felt, contemplating this anti-communist crusade, like an alcoholic contemplating the bottle. He had told Arthur Schlesinger what would happen in Vietnam: "The troops will march in ... then we will be told we have to send in more troops. It's like taking a drink, the effect wears off and you have to have another."

For a man slipping into disaster, and pulling his country with him, Ireland usefully blurred the issues. In Wexford town, he warned communist oppressors everywhere that they would "do well to remember Ireland" and its long and ultimately successful fight against "foreign domination". In this rhetoric, he could, for a while, talk as the representative of a small oppressed nation rather than of a new imperial power asserting its control over Indochina. He could be Ho Chi Minh as well as John F. Kennedy, the plucky little guy standing up to the foreign bullies, as well as the imperial overlord sliding into a terrible war. No wonder he seemed to be enjoying himself.

This, too, may explain the odd clash of expectations which Kennedy's visit involved. He may have represented modernity and glamour and sophistication, but in fact his rhetoric about Ireland was of a sort that even de Valera could no longer get away with using. He talked about this "green and misty isle," a phrase he had honed on the Irish-American circuit in the 1950s. He talked about loyalty to faith and fatherland. He talked about endurance and fortitude. He talked to us as if we were plucky little South Vietnam, a God-fearing peasant people who would always be loyal and always endure.

He didn't seem to know that what we wanted was to drive cars like his, to wear dark glasses like his, to be beautiful like him and Jackie, to be rich and happy, to shop in malls and bowl in alleys. He didn't seem to know that when he came the First Programme for Economic Expansion had just delivered increases of 20 per cent in purchasing power and wages. He didn't seem to know that in five years the rate of unemployment had dropped by 30 per cent and that in ten years the number of cars on the road had doubled. He didn't seem to know that while he was looking for a past, we were looking to him as an image of the future, that the confidence he would give us would be the confidence to outgrow our adoration of him.

There was a hint of this clash in Limerick when Frances Condell, the mayor, welcomed him by reminding him that "we have seen the introduction to Ireland of a new type of American who is taking his place in our civic and social life, and who is bringing to our people the skills and techniques of industry," and asking please could we have some more of them in Limerick. In reply, Kennedy merely did his hands-up trick and quoted the words of "Come back to Erin, mavourneen, mavourneen..." It was a silent movie and he was Valentino. We adored him, but there was no dialogue. If he had listened to the bells of Saint Nicholas Collegiate Church playing *The Star Spangled Banner* as he drove through Galway he might have understood better what faith and fatherland really meant to us.

In this confusion of desires, Kennedy created strange hybrid images of the Irish situation which mingled economic jargon and personal grief. He told us that "most countries send out oil, iron, steel or gold, some others crops, but Ireland has only one export and that is people." Later, he told us that "other nations of the world, in whom Ireland has long invested her people are now investing their capital as well as their vacations here in Ireland."

In these images of Irish people as raw materials for export, as investments in foreign economies, of tourism as a fitting return for lost families, he spoke, without meaning to, a kind of truth that no Irish leader would have dared to utter. In those brutal words, intended to be soothing, he revealed the nature of the exchange in which Ireland was involved. In the middle of all the euphoria, all the self-delusion, he killed illusions about ourselves. When the euphoria was gone, and when the self-pity which followed his assassination in Dallas had dried up, those words remained as a clear description of our place in the world. By the time his image had faded in our heads and been obscured by sex stories and conspiracy theories, he had left us that accidental legacy of unpleasant but necessary truth. We faced the world thereafter with less innocence, less gullibility, more confidence and more clarity.

2.

"Ask not what your country can do for you, " said John F. Kennedy on the morning of his inauguration "ask what you can do for your country." The ward bosses and the foot soldiers of the Irish-American political machine which had created the Kennedys as the first family probably wept into their beer at the stirring sentiments, but in their hearts of hairy bacon they knew better. Knowing precisely who did what for whom and what was given in return was the oil that made the machine work. Up in Chicago, Boss Daley may have had a flickering memory of the songs he sang on the camaign trail on the Irish South Side, getting out the vote for the man whose protégé he once was: *Whataya gonna do for McDonough?*
Whataya gonna do for YOU?
Are ya gonna carry your precint?

Are ya gonna be true blue?

Whenever ya want a favour,

McDonough was ready to do.

Whataya gonna do for McDonough,

after what he has done for you?

As the Curse of the Kennedys rides again, returning like a battered mummy in a hammered-up Hammer Horror sequel, we glimpse again the spectre of tragedy that plays about Ireland's American dream. Between the idealism and the machinery lies a genuine sorrow about what the Irish can become and the debt we owe to history that stops us from becoming very much. In America and in Ireland we made political machines to defend ourselves with, to redress the balance of starvation and injustice and bigotry. We always believed we would do something with the machines that would be worthwhile, but we ended up trapped inside them, caught between what you can do for your country and what McDonough can do for you. The Kennedys are the ghosts in the Irish political machine. The tragedy is that the same machine that has delivered much of what is best in American politics in the last three decades, can also turn its hand to digging up the dirt on a woman who says she was raped.

The great Irish contribution to politics is not any particular set of ideas but the political machine. It was born out of desperation and destitution, out of Daniel O'Connell and the Famine and No Irish Need Apply. The Irish must be one of the few peoples who had a highly sophisticated political system before they ever had a state. We had it in New York and Chicago and Boston, where the first Irish Boss, "Mahatma" Lomasney, met the wretched immigrants on the wharves and offered them a deal: "Is somebody out of a job? We do our best to place him, and not necessarily on the public payroll. Does the family run in arrears with the butcher or the landlord? We lend a helping hand. Do the kids need clothing or the mother a doctor? We do what we can and, sure, as the world is run, such things must be done. We keep old friends and make new ones."

In return, you voted the way you were told to vote. Lomasney developed the famous fine-tooth comb, with the teeth cut out in a pattern that, when superimposed on the ballot paper, showed exactly how to vote. And, sure, as the world was run who could blame the Irish, when they finally got their own state, for still seeing politics as a welfare state, for retaining a mental fine-tooth comb that could be applied to the ballot paper to give the right result?

Because the Irish were denied power for so long, power became its own end, a moral virtue in itself, a redressing of old wrongs even if it was not used to redress any new ones. When Honey Fitzgerald, father of Rose Kennedy, became the first mayor of Boston whose parents had been born in Ireland, thus founding the Kennedy dynasty of power, he shed a tear in his victory speech for his dead partners: "It would have been a great delight to them for the natives of a country where democracy could not be exercised freely due to English domination."

Being Irish meant that however rich and powerful you were, you carried with you the elan of the oppressed, just as, back home, being part of the national movement meant that you didn't have to actually tackle oppression: your very presence in power was a blow against oppression.

The problem for the Kennedys, like the problem for Irish politics at home, was that of bringing to life the ghost in the machine, the spirit of real political idealism that hovered somewhere around its cogs and wheels. Could you add intellectual substance and moral commitment to the machinations, or would such nebulous things be always chewed up in the innards of the machine? While the Kennedys were taking up the cause of Martin Luther King, the great Irish machine politician whom they needed for the purposes of power, Richard J. Daley, Boss of Chicago, was making speeches attacking "psuedo-liberals, liberal intellectuals, suburban liberals, suburban liberal-intell-

ectuals, and psuedo liberal-intellectual suburbanities."
But even this attack had little of conviction about it. When
Daley was finally attacked himself at a democratic party
meeting by someone who pointed out that without the
liberals, the party would be nothing but a power hungry
skeleton, Daley brilliantly won the war before the conflict
even got under way by simply declaring: "I've always been
a liberal myself." It is a tactic that has been employed again
in post-Robinsonian Ireland. The machine is neutral: to
survive it will learn to love the goals it has previously
despised. For it knows that there is really no goal but
power.

Because of all this, the story of the Kennedys can never
be merely what Peter Collier and David Horowitz call it in
the subtitle to their book on the family: "An American
Drama". It must also be, as they acknowledge in the first
sentence of *The Kennedys*, "an Irish tale" — a tale which
goes back nearly 300 years to the day when a woman
named Goody Glover was hanged as a witch on Boston
Common because she'd knelt in front of the Blessed Virgin
while telling her rosary beads in the "devils tongue" of
Gaelic. The question which the Kennedy saga poses —
whether the Irish political machine can ever drag itself
away from its origins in the naked manipulation of power
— is very much an Irish question, alive in the Ireland of
1991.

The Kennedys embody the Irish dream and the Irish
nightmare. To go from the Mick Alleys and Paddyvilles of
New York, Chicago and Boston to Palm Beach and
Hyannisport, from Famine Irish to the White House before
you can say (as Rose Kennedy was heard to say in the early
days) "When will the nice people of Boston accept us?" is
the dream. To be dragged back down by the savage Mick
that the nice people of Boston always knew was inside you,
by the sex and drink and deathly urge to get one over on
the other guy, is the nightmare.

In the dream, we get to the top on behalf of all the alienated and despised and discriminated against races and nations. In the nightmare, we set our lawyers and dectectives on the reputations of lower-class women who have dared to cross us. The dream still has enormous power in this country — if you are serving burgers in the Bronx, you are a potential Kennedy, if you are serving burgers in Castlebar, you are an actual nobody. We need the periodic re-emergence of the nightmare to remind us that the machine is not always a dream machine.

Maybe we need to wake up from the Kennedy dream before we can begin to get properly disillusioned with the Machine and all its works. We still use the old Irish-American title for the head of the machine — Boss. And we still have the illusion that somehow or other a Kennnedy can emerge from the Machine, full of hope and idealism and generosity. Remembering that even the real Kennedys find it imposssible to fully emerge, we should perhaps be a little more sceptical.

Or maybe, we will just accept the Machine as it is and forget the dream altogether. Last year, a new restaurant opened in Dublin called after one of the legendary figures of Irish-American machine politics, Boss Croker. And just last weekend I wandered into another restaurant on Stephen's Green. On one wall was an enormous shrine with a huge portrait surrounded by the American colours. The portrait was of Mayor Richard J. Daley of Chicago, the Boss himself.

3.

Just after the second World War, while the United Nations was being formed and the post-war world was taking shape, John F. Kennedy went to Hollywood with his friend Chuck Spalding, who worked as an assistant to Gary Cooper.

There were parties and starlets and drinking sessions. Much more important, though, there were ideas beginning to shape themselves in the future president's head. As he watched Gary Cooper and Clark Gable and Jean Tierney, Kennedy became fascinated "by the way ordinary people came to inhabit the extraordinary celluloid identities created for them."

As Spalding remembered it, "Charisma wasn't a catchword yet, but Jack was very interested in that blinding magnetism these screen personalities had. What exactly was it? How did you go about acquiring it? Did it have an impact on your private life? How did you make it work for you? He couldn't let the subject go."

Due to the fascination which Ronald Reagan's background as a Hollywood actor engendered, it was easily forgotten that, however much Reagan represented an elision of real politics with screen fantasy, Kennedy had been there first and had achieved something much more profound. Reagan was a bad actor who became a bad president, but Kennedy was a man who set out to shape politics as a celluloid fiction.

His father had been a movie mogul, a creator of industrial fantasies, where Reagan had been a mere B-movie actor. Kennedy created first a literary, then a cinematic image of himself. He won the presidency partly because he looked so much better on screen than Richard Nixon did. And, even before his death, he was played by an actor in a movie version of a real incident from his own life: "PT 109".

Kennedy created an amalgam of fiction and reality in his own image which was so powerful that it has become stronger with the passage of time. In Dublin in March, 1992 you could have read a big splash in the *Sunday Press* linking the deaths of Kennedy and of the screen idol Marilyn Monroe in a manner which, however dubious it might be as fact, seems unassailably appropriate as image.

104

You could then have gone to *Conversations on a Homecoming* at the Abbey, a play haunted, not by Kennedy but by the image of Kennedy as embodied in the tantalisingly absent figure JJ Kilkelly, his small-town Irish imitator. And you could have gone to the Irish premiere of Oliver Stone's *JFK*, a film which takes the confusion of fiction and reality in the Kennedy image to yet further heights.

Kennedy's assassination, in itself, is the defining moment of the shift from the modern to the post-modern, from a relatively stable sense of the difference between art and life on the one hand, to the media culture which we now inhabit, in which we experience reality through electronic and celluloid media which constitute it as a work of art.

The reason we return to John Kennedy's death, and not to Robert's, is that John's is on television. When we run it through our heads, we run it in slow motion, in lurid newsreel colours. The bullet hitting his cavalcade is the inauguration of the media age, the first moment of history that is shared by everyone because it can be seen by everyone, over and over again.

It is significant that this sense of one cultural age passing and another being inaugurated was felt directly artists. The playwright Arthur Miller puts it most succinctly in his autobiography *Timebends*: "Even in the Thirties, as bad as things got, there was always the future; certainly in all my work was an implicit reliance on some redemptive time to come, a feeling that the cosmos cared about man, if only to mock him. With Kennedy's assassination, the cosmos had simply hung up the phone."

To this death of an era there have been two kinds of artistic response. One, following on from Miller's sense of the loss of meaning, has been to see in Kennedy's death the image of a mocking kind of despair, the absurdity of catastrophe happening but the world going on as normal, failing to die when it so patently should. That is the feeling which runs through Tom Murphy's *Conversations on a Homecoming*. It is also the sense of Robert Patrick's play *Kennedy's Children*. Thomas Kinsella, in his poem for the 10th anniversary of Kennedy's death, *The Good Fight*, compares the world after the assassination —

...a fish,

flung back, that lay stunned,

shuddered into consciousness,

and dived back into the depths ...

That sense that what the world returned to after the shock of Kennedy's death was "the depths" is, nevertheless, a reaction which makes sense only in the old world — the world where history is made up of events, and events are real, and real things change the world. There is, though, another kind of response, elicited both by the fact that Kennedy was an image as much as he was a real person and by the power of his death as a media image rather than as history.

This response relates to a different, post-modern world, one where history is made up of images and images are infinitely recyclable and nothing ever changes.

The great American artist Robert Rauschenberg already used photographs of Kennedy in his 1960s "combine paintings", along with eagles, ropes and bits of rag: Kennedy was an object which could be made into a work of art, a part of the melding of art and reality that was central to Rauschenberg's strategy: "My works have the value of reality....my combine paintings are actual."

As, in post-modern culture, history comes to be regarded as a storehouse of images rather than a record of events, the historical event of Kennedy's assassination is converted into *The Book of Genesis* of the media world, the great point at which real events became free-floating images, there to be used and re-used regardless of any historical meaning.

This sense of Kennedy's death as above all a photograph or technological image of reality itself reaches its zenith in Don DeLillo's superb novel *Libra*, which blends invention and reality with breathtaking skill.

Here is DeLillo's description of the assassination: "A woman with a camera turned and saw that she was being photographed. A woman in a dark coat was aiming a Polaroid right at her. It was only then she realised she'd just seen someone shot in her own viewfinder." Jack Ruby watches the killing over and over again on television: "it was almost as though they were re-enacting the crucifixion of Jesus."

That sense of re-enactment dovetails with Arthur Miller's more conventional, if more despairing reaction — the feeling that there was now no future, and that our sense of time and history is out of joint. Where there is no future tense, the past tense and the present tense don't quite work either.

The endless, numbing return to the moment of Kennedy's assassination, the obsessive search for theories that will fill the black holes of that static darkness, is the mark of a culture that has nowhere to go but round in circles.

4.

There is a strange optimism about conspiracy theories. In spite of the dark mutterings, the invisible hands, the malign forces that control our destinies, the world of the conspiracy is a paradoxically comforting one. The conspiracy is the God of a Godless world. God may not be in his heaven, but someone after all, is up there controlling things, making things happen, giving a shape to an otherwise terrifyingly random world.

Believing that the awful violence and chaos of the world you live in is merely what it appears to be is a sickening kind of disillusion. Being able to trace in those events the work of an evil mind or minds relieves that pain. There is, as we know in Ireland a strong connection between the religious mind and the conspiratorial psyche: God and the conspiracy stem from the same need to see an order amidst chaos.

It is this connection which gives Oliver Stone's remarkable film *JFK* its ecstatic, almost religious quality. In that painful ecstasy, fact and fiction, history and invention, are distinctions which cease to matter.

JFK is paradoxical in other, more direct matters of form and content. On the one hand there is the *JFK* which is probably the most profound incursion of the technologies and attitudes of pop video, even of experimental "art" video, into the mainstream cinema. There is the almost literally stunning sensory overload, the speed of the camera and the editing deceiving not merely the eye but the brain.

We move between not two but three layers of reality — actual documentary footage, fiction film and, most disturbing, reinvented documentary film: scenes we are familiar with from television news film, but which have been re-staged with a disorientating mixture of period accuracy and anachronistic technological representation.

While this is happening to your eyes something analogous is being done to your ears, pounded as they are by a sound track in which "natural" sounds like the revving of engines or the scything of plants melt indistinguishably into the pounding of drums or the rattle of maracas. Even the more conventional musical aspects of the score create this same sense of the confusion of opposites, with the stately tones of the great Irish lament *Marbhna Luimni* inextricably interwoven with Latin American percussion.

In the midst of this barrage of the senses, you sit awed and numbed like a devotee at a religious ritual, entranced and mesmerised as the screen circles back and back again to the sacred moment of the assasination.

Yet interwoven with this strange avant-garde film of dislocation and disorientation is another movie, one which is conventional to the point of sentimentality and nostalgia. Where the first movie is stunningly futuristic in its form, this second one is incredibly nostalgic in its content. It is Frank Capra revisited, a remake of *Mr. Smith Goes to Washington* (1939).

Kevin Costner's Jim Garrison is Jimmy Stewart as the small-town lawyer taking on the Washington establishment. Costner indeed, plays not so much Garrison as Stewart. There is the same slow drawl, the same innocent perplexity at the evils of the world, the same appeal to good old fashioned middle-American patriotism. The supreme irony of *JFK* is that it is this good old-fashioned American movie, and not the weird technological post-modern movie that is interwoven with it, that causes the profound political unease about the confusion of history and intention which the film induces.

For me at least, the intercuttings and the editings, the obsessive returns to and reinventions of the assassination itself, are the parts of *JFK* which ring most true. This is so not in spite of the fact that they play dazzling games with the idea of what is real, but because of it. There is a genuine sort of truth in the sense of disorientation which they induce, and in their location of the beginning of that sense of disorientation in the moment of assassination. The assassination does mark the inauguration of a post-modern world of confusion between media and reality, and I know of no better evocation of that aspect of our world than *JFK*.

This radical and stunning evocation of what it is like to live in the western world now, is, unfortunately, not enough for Oliver Stone. He also wants to evoke the feeling of a pre-lapsarian American Utiopia before the fall of the assassination. The side of *JFK* which is seeking to recreate the world of Frank Capra — decent, God-fearing, good-living men who stood up for truth in a society that, however corrupt, would ultimately be unable to resist their idealism — is, ironically, the one which is most economical with the truth. In making *Mr. Garrison Goes To Washington*, Stone has to conform to the demands of the genre. And the main demand of the genre is that Jimmy Stewart has to be not merely good but right. Jim Garrison has to be right.

Stone had available to him a story that would have avoided the pitfalls he stumbles into. Garrison could still have been the centre of the movie, could still, even, have been an archetypally good man. The story of a good man trying to locate himself within a world where reality has become unattainable, a man becoming ever more obsessive and even further from discovering the key to what he is trying to discover, would have matched Stone's methods.

At times, Stone seems close to making this movie. But the essential conservatism of his vision, requiring as it does the symbol of an older purer America, imposes the need for a Garrison who is not a good man descending into madness in his pursuit of a truth, but a man who is right in all things, whose theories have to be endorsed. Thus even though the evidence of the film itself suggests that Garrison's prosecution of Clay Shaw is a show trial and an abuse of justice, it has to be presented as a great moral crusade.

This conservatism has its nasty side, too. Stone's vision of a good, decent America is articulated in the film through a dangerously simplistic set of contrasting images. The good guys are handsome, normal-looking and rooted in the nuclear family. The bad guys are peculiar-looking, physically imperfect and homosexual.

And Stone uses these contrasts with a chilling brilliance in which physical and sexual normality become moral categories rather than merely descriptive facts. In his rage at what America has become, Stone draws on both the benign decency of an older America and its dangerous and claustrophobic simplicities.

Hung as it is between a nostalgic past tense and a futuristic vision of society, between *Mr. Smith Goes to Washington"* and *1984*, *JFK* is a powerful document of a time which feels itself to have only a past tense and a future tense, but no present tense, no stable point in the present from which to define itself.

The film's tragedy though, is that it ends up being not a critique of this condition, but a stunning example of it.

KICK THE CAN

The thin steel cut into the ice, like a knife into a wedding cake, sending invisible furrows of white powder to each side of the skate. Billows of smoke rose towards the ceiling of the church, incense scented charcoal, as the altar boy swung the thurible. Squeals of delight echoed round the cold quarry as the children hurled themselves over the frozen surface of the bottomless pit. Murmurs of prayer ascended with the steam from their wet coats, and the priest prepared to raise his hands in benediction. There was one crack and then two screams as the children disappeared into the open mouth of the ice. Murmers of unease rippled through the congregation as the priest was called from the altar and returned to mount the pulpit steps, his face set in plaster like a death-mask. A last glimpse of a small hand vanished, sucked into the dark, relentless water. "Go home," said the priest "and check on your children. There has been a terrible accident in the quarry pool."

These images threatened the tranquillity of the morning as we wound our way round the edge of the cycle track, a hollow in the middle of the park that had once been the quarry pool and was now officially called Eamonn Ceannt Stadium in memory of one of the leaders of the 1916 Rising. I saw it now, its grey tarmacadam sides sloping outwards like the ashen rim of an extinct volcano and remembered it as it had been a few weeks before splashed with the roaring red jerseys of the Russian cyclists, red as erupting lava, bringing that same volcano to life. I remembered the wonder of that evening, those exotic red centaurs, half-men, half-machines, making the whole cycle track spin like a whipped top as they hurtled round, suspended at impossible angles by invisible wires of centrifugal force.

And I remembered, too, going home that evening and telling my mother where I had been and she remembering the night she had been on retreat in the church and the priest announcing the terrible news about the children drowned in the quarry. I touched the wire of the fence surrounding the track and found it cold against my clammy fingers, much colder than the summer morning air.

We were going through the estate of Crumlin on our way to Terenure to find bamboos. There was something awesome about a bamboo, its feel as smooth as a bleached white bone, the incredible contrast between its innocent weightlessness in the hand and the burning sting it could deliver to the flesh, the way it could divide the very air with a singing whish. Bamboos had grace and danger and we desired them that summer with a maddening lust. Johnny Connolly, who had assumed leadership of our shifting, ill-defined gang, said that he had seen bamboos in the garden of a big house in Terenure and that morning we fell into line for the expedition.

Johnny had the authority of absence. For eight days once he had disappeared from home and school. His picture had been printed in the evening paper, along with a description of the clothes he had last been seen wearing and a request to contact the police. His absence had hung about the place like a lost dog. True, kids often disappeared, a few dying, a few emigrating, but mostly just sent to Letterfrack or Artane for mitching school or knocking off a few pence. They would vanish, the word of where they had been sent would spread, and they would return, quieter, sneakier, more vicious. But Johnny's missing days were more mysterious, redolent as they were of a thousand dark possibilities. Fantastic rumours had been traded in the park shelters: he had been ritually murdered by satanists in the Hell Fire Club, which we could see clearly in the hilly distance; he had done a bunk with the poor box out of the chapel; and there was something about girls which I had to pretend to understand. Eventually, a man in Bray recognised him and he was sent home. His refusal to say

113

anything about what he had done and where he had gone was so absolute that by now we had given up asking. But when he suggested going to look for bamboos, there was no one, not even one as timid as me, who could resist.

I did not think it consciously as we trailed through the estate, through the winding, treeless monotonous roads flanked by rows of identical little houses in blocks of four or eight, dodging children playing Beds with shoe polish boxes for piggies, and dogs that might dart out of occluded gateways, but we were children of a new wilderness. We were city kids but our games were different from those of our parents who grew up nearer to the city centre. We could play football on the roads. We could use Alsatians to hunt rats in the dank darkness under the canal bridges. We had a game specifically invented for the narrow roads of the estate, where you threw a ball from the path on one side and scored a point if it ricocheted back into your arms off the sharp edge of the opposite path. By growing up where we did we were different from them, though we shared something of their sense of loss.

Like us that day, our parents had been explorers, though for the most part involuntary ones, cast adrift without map or compass, deprived of familiar co-ordinates, thrust, as Jim Larkin put it in 1939 "into areas to which they are not acclimatised". "They are simply dumped down there; they don't understand their surroundings. No one ever goes near them except to collect the rent." To many the very air that they breathed in Crumlin seemed literally alien and dangerous. Larkin complained that people with tuberculosis were being put into Crumlin and ran a campaign on behalf of a man who had been allocated a house in Lismore Road even though he had TB: "The atmosphere there was such that this man with TB could not stand it." To the planners, the fresh clean air of Crumlin was to be a blessing for the labouring classes after their confinement in the grimy atmosphere of the city centre, but for the poor who were planted in Crumlin the reality was different. "A lot of people," admitted Dublin Corporation's Allocations Officer Thomas Burke in 1939 "declare that the air is so strong that the children eat them out of house and home. They cannot afford to keep the children in food. They would prefer to go back to any place out of it."

If even the air was an alien element, Crumlin had little history or legend to locate yourself by, and what it had belonged to those other than our parents' tribe, the Catholic Irish, to invaders and aliens, outlanders and outlaws. The invading Partholans settled here and buried their plague victims nearby. Oisin, not the vigorous hero of the Fianna, but the dying returned exile, shaking his head and mumbling about the changed times, had lived here, alone, afraid, confused. King Billy had issued a proclamation prohibiting the use of brass money from Crumlin, an act still celebrated in the oath of the Orange Order, but celebrated only by the infidel Protestant. Holinshed's *Chronicles* had described the rabble of Crumlin as a "lobbish and desperate clobberiousness". Such scraps of esoteric history, even had they known them, could not have served as fixed co-ordinates for Crumlin's new people, disparate, desperate, uprooted and ungrateful as they were.

We straggled along Sundrive Road. Here the planners who had ordained this place had performed their first act of faith, animated by a naïve belief in the word magic. They had taken a serpentine mud track called The Dark Lane and transformed it by the power of words into Sundrive Road, a nomenclature that summoned up the beatific bourgeois vision of happy families out for a jaunt on a sunny Sunday afternoon, a propitious place to build the houses for the first ninety families to occupy in 1935. On moving in, they found that other Victorian visions had come into play: houses specifically designed for very large families had just two small bedrooms, and yet the designers had seen fit to take up precious space with that most Victorian of bourgeois domestic ideals — a parlour. ("Somewhere" an old lady told me "to bring the insurance man for a chat when somebody died.") Nor could the planners bring themselves to see the houses as places of work: the kitchens were combined with the main living area, leaving the working women with no space of their own and large families under their feet. "Somebody told me," said Dominic Behan, who lived on Kildare Road, "that the man responsible for their design committed suicide. I'm quite sure his death, if at all, was accidental, for no man with a mind like his could ever succeed in anything so calculated as taking a life, even his own."

The Crumlin through which we made our way was an intemperate remark, not fully uttered before being deeply regretted. Conceived in panic, born of haste, and raised in rueful dismay, Crumlin was not fully built before officials and institutions were already talking of it as a mistake. Within a year of the first families moving in, the Society of Saint Vincent de Paul had issued an urgent appeal, stating that many of Crumlin's tenants had great difficulty in affording the rents, as well as additional busfares and that this had caused "serious reduction in the amount of food which could be bought." "Many families find it impossible under present conditions to live, save on a level that amounts practically to starvation." A District Justice McCarthy, sentencing young men of the area, was soon to ask "Does anything good ever come out Crumlin?" Even the City Engineer and Town Planning Officer had jointly suggested that the policy of "providing very large areas of single-class housing" should not be repeated. "It is hardly necessary to emphasise the difficulties that have resulted from this policy which has given us large areas of one-class communities as Crumlin." Hardly had they been invented when Crumlin and its people had been virtually written off and written out.

For in spite of the cheery optimism which transformed Dark Lane into Sundrive Road, Crumlin was the product more of fear and shame than of idealism. The shame lay in the fact that Independent Ireland, having blamed British neglect for the degradation of the Dublin tenements had itself, if anything, presided over a worsening in the housing conditions of the Dublin working-class. In 1913, there were 25,822 Dublin families living in conditions unfit for human habitation, making the city the scandal of Europe. In 1938, the figure was actually higher: 28,210 families, nearly 70,000 people.

And this shame bred fear, fear of disorder, fear of breakdown, fear of chaos. In 1939, Dublin Corporation's Housing Allocations Officer reported that tension over housing allocation could lead to "riots in the city": "At first, when I took over, the city of Dublin area was in a very discontented state...Members of the Council were actually knocked down." As late as 1945, the Jesuit periodical Studies noted that "There is in Dublin a growing population of Christians who have not succeeded in resisting the horrible pressure of rats, filth and overcrowding and who are losing, generation by generation, their traditional standards of human decency...dressed in rags, inarticulate, dirty, and often dishonest, they drift into the street corner gangs which are the despair of social workers and the concern of the police. This class of social pariahs, existing on inadequate relief...already constitutes a social danger which might easily grow to uncontrollable dimensions."

With fear, came compulsion. Most of the people who settled in Crumlin were forced to do so. Their own slum areas, zoned for clearance, were demolished, the Corporation fulfilling its obligations by shifting the people to Crumlin. For the Corporation, houses in Crumlin cost just six hundred pounds each to build, compared to nine hundred in the city centre. (Decent houses in Crumlin would have cost more: when the Iveagh Trust built good working-class homes in Crumlin in 1925, the houses cost them nine hundred and fifty one pounds each to build.)

People were forced from slum rooms at five shillings a week in the city centre to houses in Crumlin that cost between seven shillings and sixpence and ten shillings a week. In addition there was an extra half crown busfares a week for every working member of the family, all coming from an income that was generally around two pounds and ten shillings. For a very large proportion of its population, therefore, Crumlin was an immediate disaster, a calamity that had descended on them in their innocence. "I know," said Thomas Burke of the Corporation "that if we have to clear an area, none of the families will go outside the area. There may be an odd family that will go out to Crumlin." Of those who did not want to go to Crumlin "in most of these cases we decide they have to go off to Crumlin."

The degree of compulsion is clear from the Corporation's own surveys of its tenantry. A survey in the late thirties of 20,000 families living in overcrowded accommodation in the city centre — people who were, therefore, living in desperate conditions — which offered them houses in Crumlin and Larkhill as the "only two schemes in which they would have any chance" of Corporation housing, got a total of 360 applicants for Crumlin and 200 for Larkhill. "That means" concluded Burke "that at the present moment those people in the city do not want to go to Larkhill or Crumlin at all."

And acquaintance with Crumlin did nothing to assuage the feelings of being in internal exile. In 1939, just four years after the first tenants moved in, Burke was forced to admit that 400 of the 2,000 families had actually applied to be transferred back to the city centre. "We did not grant any at all." And even this figure of 20% of the population which was prepared to move back to slum conditions was a gross underestimate. "To others who would apply we would say "it is no use in applying unless you get someone else to exchange. If we were to circularise the Crumlin tenants, and ask them how many would like to get back to the city, we would get a thousand applications. They would get the impression that they could get back, and a regular landslide would take place. For that reason, we avoid asking if they would like to get back." Burke was already despairing of the possibility of housing the working-class in Crumlin without outright compulsion. "They were asked would they go to Crumlin; they said 'Crumlin will do us all right.' Then they come back and say 'Crumlin would suit you but it does not suit me at all.' ... They feel out of their element, and the sooner they get back, they think, the better... we will eventually have to reach a point where we will have to force these people into these houses."

The Crumlin they created was, to a large extent, a city of children and consumptives. Families with tuberculosis and families with large numbers of children were given priority in the allocation of housing, so that these two types of maltreated humanity prevailed. And for the first fifteen years of the estate's life, before the virtual eradication of TB in the city, the consumptives infected the children. One doctor noted of Crumlin in 1945 that "persons suffering from active pulmonary tuberculosis" were "sprinkled at random throughout a community of babies, young children, and adolescents, when they were at their most infective stage and their unfortunate young neighbours at the most susceptible period of their lives. No tuberculosis dispensary, no hospital, not even a district nurse at first, were provided to mitigate this evil." And children died, their corpses added to the underground history that Crumlin was accumulating.

For those children who lived, a fine facility was provided for their future, a magnificent granite police barracks overlooking the estate, easily Crumlin's finest building until the permanent church was erected. "A *fine police barracks,*"Studies noted wryly in 1945 "has been provided to control the unruly crowds of workless adolescents for whom there are no factories, no technical schools, no secondary schools, no football grounds."

119

We left the estate and edged towards the lusher gardens, the more spacious and sedate houses of Terenure. We climbed walls, jumped over streamlets, crawled through thickets, Johnny taking us over some unknown terrain that skirted the back gardens of the rich. We plunged into a hollow and emerged again, then dropped over a high wall, the impact shooting a thud from my heels to my brain. This was it. We were in a loose copse of half-wild shrubs, interlaced with nettles and brambles, from which we could see, across a dipping stream and a rising bank, the whole grove of waving bamboos, their thin green plumes nodding in the breeze. We rushed through the copse, brambles tearing at our clothes, nettles injecting acid into our bare legs. We splashed through the shallow muddy water and in the same movement hurled ourselves up the steep bank, where at the top a man in flannel trousers with iron grey hair stood shouting "Get to hell out of here or I'll call the police." We scattered in terror, some rolling, some jumping down the bank, and when next we recollected ourselves, we were sitting in the tall grass in the field beside the graveyard, about a mile away. We sat there shocked and disconsolate for a long time, realising as we had not done before that we might have been criminals or outlaws, that we might have gone to Letterfrack, and, worse still, that we would never have bamboos.

A few nights later, my mother had a dream. In it she saw Johnny Connolly lying in our road, his life's blood draining away, his lips mouthing the words "Help me" but no one near to save him. In the morning she told us of the dream. At lunchtime when we came home from school we heard that Johnny had died. He had broken into the dispensary the previous night and shoved handfuls of coloured pills down his throat. They found him sitting in a chair, his eyes wide open, his hand stretched out in supplication. They said it had taken him a while to die. He was the first young man in our area to die of an overdose, though some years later old women would be handing out syringes and sachets of heroin to the children at the primary school gates, and at night the pebbledashed walls of the houses were flecked by the moving shadows thrown by the torches of the vigilantes.

The afternoon at school after we heard about Johnny hung about our shoulders like an old kit bag full of troubles. The clock, its heavy case stained with the accumulated exhalations of our young years, beat out time with the threatening monotony of a Christian Brother tapping his leather in agitation upon a desk. Seven minutes past three. Ten past. Thirteen past. The teacher's voices thickened to an indistinct hum, a rumble on a faraway highway, fading into some other distance. A quarter past. I closed one eye, then opened it and closed the other, making a telegraph pole flick from one window to the next, the only moving thing on the horizon. I looked into the Jewish graveyard beside the school and the white stones stared unblinkingly back.

Below, in the schoolyard, the little kids, already free, were playing kick-the-can. You put an empty can on the ground, covered your eyes and counted while the others hid. Then, one by one, they emerged with stealth or with speed to try to kick the can. If you touched them before they could kick it over, they fell down dead and lay frozen until someone managed to kick it, and it crashed across the concrete like the last trumpet blowing. Then, like good souls on the last day, their bodies would rise again in glory. This particular guardian of the can was nimble, and already young bodies were scattered, fallen around the prize.

There was a commotion from the graveyard and its green doors swung open and a crowd first filed, and then shoved in. Old Cullen the gravedigger pressed his palms together nervously and hopped from one foot to the other as he inched backwards, afraid to turn his back on the advancing dignitaries. The crowd was pierced by the brow of a coffin as it forged through like an icebreaker, borne on the shoulders of six long, thin, dark men. And there, behind the coffin, thinner, darker, made impossibly long by the black top hat that grew out of his head like the funnel of a stately ocean liner, was Him — Dev, Eamon de Valera, the Chief, the President of the Republic. I stared in shock and disbelief and then remembered that today was indeed the burial day of Robert Briscoe, a former Lord Mayor of Dublin, an old Fianna Fáil comrade-in-arms.

And as they glided silently towards the grave, I thought for some reason of the time when Brother Chalky, similarly long and just as decrepit, advancing with menace on us in the yard, had suddenly and without a sound fallen straight as a poker into an open shore, a momentary, wordless, exclamation mark. And in my daydream I saw Dev and his comrades sail majestically towards the open maw of the grave, seeing nothing in their blindness until they stumbled in and were swallowed. Down they fell, endlessly down, until the black of their clothes merged with the blackness of the earth and they were gone forever.

In the yard, a boy was gaining on the can, its guardian just behind but out of reach. I knew for that moment that he would kick it before he could be touched and that its tumultuous clatter across the concrete would awaken not just the dead of the yard, but all the dead children of Crumlin, the tubercular, the overdosed, the drowned. In the park, under the cycle track named after the hero of 1916, the ice would part again, and small hands would grasp its sides. The skaters would climb out, shake the cold drops from their backs, and go home. His foot was poised to strike and the tin can glinted in the still strong sun. "Kick the can," I shouted in my mind. "Kick the fucking can."

Religion

MIXED BLESSINGS

The end of the Irish Church

In English, the days of the week take their names from a curiously promiscuous collection of gods, Roman, Viking, and Pagan, from Saturn to Woden to the Moon. In Irish, three days are named after, not Gods, but penitential religious practices. The Irish for Wednesday translates as "first fast," for Friday as "the fast," and for Thursday as "the day between the two fasts". Wednesday and Friday were, in the great Irish monasteries, days of fasting and mortification. Thus, in Ireland, the everyday has been literally defined, not by wandering gods, but by religious practice. For much of Irish history, the sacred and the secular have been virtually indistinguishable.

Catholicism in Ireland has long been a nationality as much as a religion. The words "Irish Catholic" do not denote merely a person of a specific faith born in a specific country. They have also come to stand for some third thing born out of the fusion of the other two — a country, a culture, a politics. Catholicism in Ireland has been a matter of public identity more than of private faith, and the struggle to disentangle the two is what defines the Irish Church now.

In Ireland, as in some other atypical European countries, such as Poland and Croatia, where political nationality was often tenuous or submerged, the Church became a kind of surrogate State, the only organised and institutionalised expression of nationality. Modern

Ireland, in its attempt to become a European republican democracy, has had to struggle with the fact that the Church was there before the State, that it can claim, and often has claimed prior rights over the territory. The State is young and fragile, with only 70 years behind it. The Church is old and seasoned, so old that its language and culture, its imagery and its power, have seeped into the society.

It is not just a matter of a strongly religious culture, though it remains true that Ireland is exceptionally religious by the standards of the western world. More people attend church once a week in Ireland (86 per cent of the overwhelmingly Catholic population) than in any other Judeo-Christian society in the world. Asked how important God is in their lives, the Irish come out far ahead of any nation in Europe. When it comes to belief in the existence of the soul, in life after death, in heaven, in prayer, the Irish score so much higher in surveys than the rest of the developed world as to seem not part of that world at all. Yet even this is not what is at issue, for such things remain, however deeply held, still matters of private belief.

It is the public nature of Catholicism in Ireland that has really marked it off. The founding act of the modern Irish State — the 1916 Rising — is a religious as much as a political act, and conceived by its leader, Patrick Pearse, as such. Its symbolic occurrence at Easter, its conscious imagery of blood sacrifice and redemption, shaped a specifically Catholic political consciousness that belied the secular republican aims of many of the revolutionaries. Irish nationalism, the primary driving force of Irish politics for most of this century, became, in both its constitutional and its violent manifestations, intimately entwined with Catholicism. Eamon de Valera saw fit to get John Charles McQuaid, the Catholic Archbishop of Dublin, to help him to write the Constitution. In the early 1980s, IRA prisoners in Northern Ireland staged a hunger strike

124

whose imagery and effect were inextricable from the penitential and martyrological traditions of Irish Catholicism.

In less directly political ways, too, the Church had an enormous public presence. The sociologist Tom Inglis has pointed out that in Ireland it was the Catholic Church which, in the nineteenth century, taught the peasant Irish not merely what to believe but how to behave. It was the Church which took an agricultural people used to landscape and the rhythms of the farming day, and taught them how to inhabit public spaces and respect modern, industrialised time-keeping. Forms of behaviour and control were inculcated by the Church in a manner which went far beyond the spiritual and into the realms of secular time and space.

And if the Church "civilised" the Wild Irish, it also provided the trappings of a State where there was no State. The Church succesfully outmanoeuvred the British government's attempts to construct a secular education system, and built its own mass education system under the control of religious brothers and nuns. It founded its own universities and hospitals. An Irish person was, and is, likely to be born in a Catholic hospital, educated at Catholic schools, married in a Catholic church, have children named by a priest, be counselled by Catholic marriage advisors if the marriage runs into trouble, be dried out in Catholic clinics for the treatment of alcoholism if he or she develops a drink problem, be operated on in Catholic hospitals, and be buried by Catholic rites. The "cradle to grave" attention of European social welfare systems was created in Ireland by the Church.

Having built all of these institutions as alternatives to British rule, the Church retained them in an Independent Ireland, and remains a massive temporal power, controlling most of the health and education systems and having a large influence in all other social services. Most primary schools are in Church ownership, as are 90 per cent of secondary schools. Teacher training is Church controlled, as are most of the training hospitals in which nurses and doctors are formed. In a real and immediate sense, the Church has successfully interposed itself between the personal worlds of education (mind) and illness (body) on the one hand, and the impersonal world of State services and institutions on the other. Holding that ground has given it enormous temporal, as well as spiritual, power.

Yet this great monolith is not all that it seems. The Irish Catholic Church is also a troubled institution, suffering a serious loss of authority. Its very strengths throughout the centuries have also become weaknesses in the Ireland of the 1990s. It is afflicted with a paradoxical problem: it cannot hope to retain power without giving up power. Two of its greatest bulwarks have become barriers.

The first strength that is now becoming a weakness lies in the very nature of Irish Catholicism itself. It achieved and retained its power through the centuries not by being simply the rock of Peter, but by being something much more like a geological section in which layer after layer of rock is submerged beneath the surface. It grew and consolidated itself not by obliterating what was there before, but by adding another layer to its surface.

Early Irish Christianity, for instance, flourished not by wiping out the earlier celtic beliefs, but by adapting them. To this day, the annual pilgrimage on the last Sunday in July up Croagh Patrick mountain in Mayo re-enacts the worship of the mountain gods in a Catholic context. Early Irish christian spirituality is marked by both the intimacy of a tribal society and by a use of natural imagery bordering on pantheism. John Scotus Eriugena (the name meaning John the Irishman, born in Eire), the greatest philosopher and theologian of the early Middle Ages, was indeed accused of pantheism, his great book *De Divisione Naturae* burned by order of the Council of Paris in 1210, and placed on the Vatican index in 1685.

These stresses on the "Irish" part of "Irish Catholicism" are best summed up in the famous Irish mediaeval monastic poem:

Who to Rome goes

Much labour, little profit knows.

For God, on earth though long you've sought him,

You'll miss at Rome unless you've brought him.

This tendency to localism and independence, to build on what is in Ireland rather than on a simple universalism, helped Irish Catholicism to survive persecution and isolation under centuries of British rule. But it also forged a kind of Catholicism that is highly dependent on the nature of Irish society. So long as the society remained relatively stable, this rootedness was a huge strength. But, in a shifting society, the Church's very close relationship to the place and the people means that the Church feels the pressure of change even more intimately than would otherwise be the case.

At a popular level, and often to the discomfort of the Catholic hierarchy, the early kind of Pagan Catholicism remains very much alive. In many rural areas, acts of devotion at, for instance, Holy Wells, vestigial shrines of forgotten water spirits, survive in a christianised form. From time to time, too, there are outbreaks of superstitious enthusiasm, such as the craze for "moving" statues of the Blessed Virgin which swept much of the country in 1985 and 1986. In some places, such as Knock, in County Mayo, visited by Pope John Paul II in 1979, this religion of magic has been fully institutionalised by the Church. But in others, it remains on the fringe of Catholicism, barely accommodated by a church all too aware of its capacity to take on a life of its own.

The modern Irish Church, however, was built in the nineteenth century by the imposition on this native layer of religion of a particularly harsh and autocratic combination of sexual puritanism and centralised bureaucracy. Both owed their success to the trauma of famine, the catastrophe of the mid-19th century which halved the population in a few decades. Because the famine had been caused at least in part by over-population, the new combination of French Jansenism and English Puritanism which the Church adopted made a kind of bitter economic sense and eventually led to a situation in the 1950s where Ireland had the lowest marriage rate in the world.

At the same time, the institutionalisation of the Church as an obedient, highly organised, highly efficient bureaucracy, also had economic roots in the Church's position after the Famine as one of the few sources of wealth and development and social services that the Catholic Irish had. On the one hand, the jobs of priest and nun provided an acceptable economic status for surplus children. On the other, the massive church and school building programmes undertaken in the latter half of the 19th century were Ireland's form of infrastructural development.

A religion that had been local, intimate and more spiritual than devotional, became a massively effective power structure. Between 1850 and 1900, Mass attendance rose from an estimated 30-40 per cent to the 90 per cent level which it retained up to the 1980s. But, as the Redemptorist priest Fr. John J. O 'Riordain has put it "The whole progress of the nineteenth century in Ireland, with its renewal of church structures, training of clergy, building of churches, expansion of religious life, and devotional revolution, might well be seen as one triumphal march. But the truth, to my mind, is less flattering. Success there was beyond doubt. But the progress was not so much earned as gained in a somewhat dishonest manner. At best it was a display of wealth by somebody who had received a legacy."

That legacy, though, lasted well into the 1980s. The groundwork laid down in the 19th century was the basis for the Church's triumph in independent Ireland. Once there was an Irish state, it became the effective arbiter of social legislation, having a ban on divorce inserted into the Constitution, encouraging the introduction of draconian censorship of books and films, delaying the legalisation of artificial contraception until 1979, retaining largely unquestioned control over schools and hospitals funded by the taxpayer, resisting the slow development of a welfare state.

Yet this very success also carried the seeds of failure. Simply because its triumph was so complete, the Irish Catholic Church did not have to develop the kind of complex lay culture which the Catholic Church built in other European Catholic countries like France and Spain and Italy.

Because the media was mostly very respectful of the Church, there was no need for specifically Catholic newspapers or broadcasting stations. Because the trade unions were only marginally "infested" by Marxism or secular radicalism, there was no need for specifically Catholic trade unions. Because all of the functioning political parties were fundamentally Catholic, there was no need for a specifically Catholic political party. Thus, Ireland, the most unequivocally Catholic society in Europe, has none of these things to this day.

Essentially, the Catholic Church exercised its power at the top and at the bottom, but not in the middle of the social process. At the top, there were secret meetings with Government Ministers and political leaders at which the Church could exercise great influence. At the bottom, there was the long-term power of controlling education and shaping minds. But in the middle, there was no genuinely Catholic intelligentsia and no Catholic civil society.

In the last decade, the top and bottom layers of influence have run into deep trouble. At the top, the Church's political influence has become steadily more marginal. The Church scored two great political victories in the 1980s, by using its influence in favour of a constitutional amendment to ban abortion and against a constitutional amendment to permit divorce. In both cases, it was on the winning side, and succeeded in holding the line against the march of secular liberalism. In both cases however, the victories were pyrrhic, achieved at the cost of a break in the politico-moral consensus that ultimately undermined the Church's authority as being "above politics". By 1990, it was possible for the leader of one of Ireland's major political parties, aligned to the Christian Democrats in Europe, to refer to an unnamed bishop in public as a "bastard".

In the case of divorce, it is now accepted as inevitable that Ireland will introduce divorce laws in the 1990s, and even the most stalwart supporter of the Church line, Fianna Fáil, has proposed to do so. In the case of abortion, the 1983 "pro-life" amendment to the Constitution recognising the right to life of the unborn foetus not only made abortion a matter of public controversy and thus increased public support for it in certain circumstances, it also led to the legalisation of abortion itself. In 1992, the Supreme Court, faced with the case of a 14-year old girl who had been raped and was pregnant and suicidal, decided that under the "pro-life" clause itself, she had the right to an abortion in Ireland.

In the subsequent referendum to roll back this judgement, the Church, for the first time in living memory, was clearly divided and marginalised, with the bishops collectively telling the faithful that they could vote either way, but individual bishops, including the powerful Archbishop of Dublin, Desmond Connell, taking a much harder line. The magesterial authority of the Church had been fatally undermined.

For different reasons, the bottom layer of influence has also become much more tenuous. Keeping control of schools and hospitals and other public services is a highly effective way of maintaining power, but it is also highly labour-intensive. It requires the kind of mass recruitment of clergy and nuns which made it possible up until the early 1970s for most Irish families to boast a member in holy orders. Such recruitment fell away almost completely during the 1970s, and has not recovered since. The shock troops of Church control in education, the Christian Brothers, are moribund, with barely enough recruits to look after the aged Brothers in retirement, never mind control and teach in hundreds of schools. Likewise most orders of nuns and priests. In the 1990s, the Church has been forced to retreat ever further into management of schools and hospitals, leaving the groundwork to lay personnel who are increasingly difficult to control.

At the same time, there are signs of increasing radicalism amongst those who do join or stay in religious orders. The extraordinary missionary tradition which sent thousands of Irish priests and nuns to a "spiritual empire" in Africa, Asia, and Latin America, has, in a sense, reversed itself, with returned missionaries importing the ideas of liberation theology and the option for the poor, ideas which threaten , rather than reinforce, the Church's place within Irish power structures.

In the 1990s, much of most radical campaigning on issues of poverty and exclusion in Ireland has come from the Conference of Major Religious Superiors, representative of the large orders of priests and nuns. When the former Taoiseach, Charles Haughey, remarked in reply to an attack from the CMRS on his economic policies that he did not trust organisations with words like "major" and "superior" in their titles, it was a mark both of the perceived incongruity of this political radicalism on the part of the Church, and of the difficulty which the political establishment often has with it.

Perhaps even more profoundly threatening to the institutional power of the Church is the quiet spread of feminism within its ranks. Nuns, for so long the obedient servants of the magesterium, have begun to threaten its authority, causing the eminent Catholic sociologist Father Liam Ryan to remark that the Church treats women like second-class citizens but must remember that "male geriatric dictatorship may well have been what finally toppled Communism in Eastern Europe."

Recognising that its power was threatened at the top and at the bottom in these ways, the Irish Church began to slowly accommodate itself to what was in the middle, the new Irish civil society which emerged from urbanisation and industrialisation in the 1960s. Early in that decade the Archbishop of Dublin, John Charles McQuaid, returning from the Second Vatican Council told his Irish flock "Allow me to reassure you, no change will worry the tranquillity of your Christian lives." By the early seventies, the Church was trying to jettison that grand paternalism and present instead the image of bishops who could sing on chat shows.

It had, however, underestimated the omnivorous power of the new media. By 1992, the bishop who was best at singing on chat shows, Bishop Eamonn Casey of Galway, appointed as the friendly face who could win through media charm the authority which the Church had previously maintained by haughty power, himself became a victim of the ultimate resistance to authority of the modern media. *The Irish Times* uncovered the fact that Bishop Casey had used diocesan funds for payments to the mother of his secret son in America. A sex scandal at the height of the Irish Catholic Church, the last unthinkable event, had happened, and the Church discovered that it could not be at one and the same time magesterial and populist, that if you tried to show a friendly face, you could not control what would in fact be revealed.

This final loss of authority has probably placed the Irish Church on an inexorable path of institutional change. It also explains why the Church cannot retain power without giving up power.

At the level of institutional, bureaucratic and political power that it attained for itself in the nineteenth century, the Irish Church is mortally wounded. Its institutions are increasingly challenged from within, and its political power, though still considerable, is rapidly on the wane. The demands of a young, highly educated population and the needs of a pluralist society to disentangle itself from the tribal religions that have made violence endemic in Northern Ireland both mean that the Church's grip on political power will continue to weaken.

But it is important to remember that it is really only this nineteenth century Church that is in sharp decline. The Church on which it imposed itself, the intimate, pantheistic and spiritual Church which had shown itself to be virtually invulnerable to persecution and poverty even if Mass attendance was relatively low, shows no sign of rapid decline. What Father Liam Ryan describes as "the four deadly sins of Irish Catholicism" — "an obesssion with sexual morality, clerical authoritarianism, anti-intellect- ualism, or at best non-intellectualism, and the creation of a ghetto mentality" — will, ironically, become less important as the faithful vote with their feet and choose simply to ignore Church teaching on sexuality, do the same with clerical authority, develop their own intellects, and step out of their ghettoes. In a sense, the more easily Irish Catholics reject the Church for its sins, the more easily will the religious culture which, like it or not, they have inherited, sit with them. The chances are that the Irish Church in the year 2000 will look remarkably like what it was in 1800 — a focus for a relaxed but deep spirituality in which the broad culture rather than the devotional and behavioural rules is what matters.

BISHOP CASEY AND THE BEGINNINGS OF MORALITY

"She prays now, she says, that I may learn in my own life, and away from home and friends, what the heart is and what it feels." That prayer of Stephen's mother, from the end of Joyce's *A Portrait of the Artist as a Young Man* is not a bad one for the present moment. What the heart is and what it feels: these are things that are learned, not taught, faced up to, not handed down. Away from home and friends, away from the securities of what we have been taught, we encounter choices. Because we don't invent those choices, because they are not abstract but real and always complicated, they are, at that moment unique. Broadly similar things have happened to others, but nobody has ever faced exactly this set of circumstances before. Yet in those choices, and only in them, morality lies. It is personal, intimate, and sometimes terrifying. And no abstract set of rules helps all that much.

In talking as they have tried to talk in the last few days, full of hurt and sorrow and vulnerability as they are, Irish Catholic bishops have been saying something like this: that we must try not to judge others, that what happened to Bishop Casey is a matter for his conscience, that none of us know the secret suffering. They are recognising, for the first time perhaps, that morality is not about a set of rules, but about the dark and difficult choices that face real people in their own hearts. They may, in this, be applying a different standard to their brother bishop than they have applied to, say Eileen Flynn or Father Bernard Lynch, but there is not necessarily anything contemptible in that.

All over the country, there are hundreds of thousands of lay Catholics who have learned to do the same thing, to come, when faced with the suffering of those close to them, to conclusions different from the ones their abstract rules would suggest. They have had to say "Sex outside marriage is wrong, but of course we'll help Mary with the baby," or "Divorce is wrong but my Johnny should be allowed to re-marry," or "I hate abortion, but Sharon just can't go through with this pregnancy." Mothers have learned that their son who stopped going to Mass isn't a bowsie. Fathers have learned that their daughter who's living with that fella isn't a tramp. These have been the moralists of modern Ireland and it has been no easier for them than it is now for the bishops. They have borne the pain and made the choices. Finally, and in the most traumatic of circumstances, their leaders have begun to follow them. Faced with the suffering of someone close to them, they have begun to learn what their faithful have learned a long time ago.

Not that they do not have a long way to go. I have yet to hear a senior churchman say what needs to be said: that a man faced with a choice between his church and his child must choose the child; that, if the bishop was guilty, his guilt lay not in loving the mother but in abandoning the son. To say that would be difficult — it would be to say that the real people are more important than the church itself and all its might and pomp. But it is not that difficult. Thousands and thousands of Irish Catholic parents have said it by going to the registry office weddings of their children, or by loving their grandchildren who are brought up in a different faith, or by welcoming their son's boyfriend to the Sunday dinner table.

If they could do it, why can't their bishops? They would, after all be doing no more than following the words of Bishop Casey himself, interviewed in 1969 when he became Bishop of Kerry: "If I were a parent I would certainly want to be very much assured... that my child was taught the truth, and not a watered-down version of it."

The evidence, however, is that not only will the bishops not say this, but that they do not believe it. David Rice, who has written so well about the human suffering of enforced celibacy, has shown us cases like that of the woman in Germany who has a child by a priest who is still in the parish but is forbidden by his bishop to acknowledge his family in public. He has also quoted from a letter sent by an American bishop to a priest who resigned in order to be a father to his children and a husband to their mother: "if you wish to return to the clerical state, you must leave your wife and children, if any, and obtain a civil divorce and do penance." If, indeed, it is episcopal policy that a clergyman who fathers a child should abandon that child in order to remain a cleric, then they are right in their feeling that they cannot judge Bishop Casey. They have no right to do so, being every bit as guilty as he might be.

There is another, wider sense in which what has happened to Bishop Casey grows out of a logic which the entire hierarchy has been involved with. In many ways what has happened to them in their attempt to combine a mystical authority with the demands of a modern media society is analagous to what has happened to the British Royal Family. In the 1960s, the Irish bishops and the British Royals were in a similar situation, trying to retain authority while being aware that authority now derived more and more from the media, particularly television.

Their first reaction to this new situation was to rail against television, as in the infamous case of *The Bishop and the Nightie* in 1966. What could and could not be said in public was still narrow enough to hope that this might actually work. When, in April 1971, just a few years before the affair between Bishop Casey and Annie Murphy, Dr Noel Browne made a speech in Tramore in which he hinted that clerical celibacy might have its ambivalences and contradictions, he was disowned by the entire Labour Party, including liberals like Conor Cruise O'Brien and

David Thornley. But slowly those limits on what could be said in Ireland were pushed further and further back.

Bishop Casey was one of the answers to this problem. Just as the Royal Family needed to let the cameras into Buckingham Palace, the hierarchy needed a bishop who could go onto the *Late Late* and sing *The West's Awake*, who could compete in the media circus on its own terms. He represented a different model of authority, one that was won in battle by force of personality. The exuberance, the energy, the colour, the impulsiveness, the very qualities which led to his downfall, were the qualities which the hierarchy so badly needed.

They needed a bishop who could win exposure, but once exposure begins, there is no way of stopping it. From singing on the *Late Late* to having your private life exposed is a short step. It is what happens to celebrities. As the Royal Family found out too late, once you let sunlight in on the magic, it fades and pales and you can never go back again to distance and mystery. The bishop as distant authority was unsustainable and the bishop as celebrity has brought disaster. What option remains?

Maybe the option of the bishop as man, fallen, fallible, ordinary, having no authority but the one that matters: the authority of experience. On the morning the story broke, just before the eight o'clock news, when many people heard it for the first time, RTE radio had a "Just a Thought" slot, given by a woman. She told the story of a woman searching for her daughter, who had become a prostitute, leaving notes for her which said "Whatever you've done, it doesn't matter. Come home." A corny story, perhaps, but one which thousands of ordinary Irish people have lived through in less dramatic ways. If the Irish bishops could manage to send such a note to their fallen brother they might, for once, be worthy of their flock. Or could it be that the sermons are meant only for the faithful, and not for the preachers too?

Irish Times, May 1992

ANNIE AND THE BISHOP, IRELAND AND AMERICA

Just before you turn off the main road towards Mullaghmore interpretative centre, now one of the most symbolic sites in Ireland, there is a ruined old church in Kilnaboy that is, in its way, yet more powerfully symbolic. Roofless and open to the elements, it has yet survived the centuries and its grey, hand-cut stones embody the unadorned endurance of the Irish Catholic church, its gravity and its ascetic beauty. Just over the doorway, though, is a sheela-na-gig, a grotesquely sexual and sternly obscene figure of a woman exposing herself. The same monks who prayed and fasted here placed this figure of terrifying womanhood at the centre of their church, a reminder, perhaps, of the flesh they had to fear and shun.

Annie Murphy is the Irish Catholic church's sheela-na-gig made flesh, an avenging spirit risen up from the dark of the celibate mind to haunt and to terrify, to embody all those dangerous thoughts subdued by prayer and fasting. She is their worst nightmare come true, a figure from the mediaeval witch-hunters' manuals: wild and indiscreet, loose-tongued and lusty. She has written a book about her love affair with a bishop, a book that is full not just of sex, but of the body itself, of beard rash and high blood pressure, of colitis and groin infections, of cancers and amputations. Of all the ills and sins that flesh is heir to.

In Irish folklore, the priest's mistress is a figure of almost supernatural evil. One old Gaelic proverb tells of "three who will never see the light of Paradise":

The angel of pride,
The unbaptised child,
And a priest's concubine.

The angel of pride is Satan. The priest's concubine (ceile shagairt) is associated with him. So, too, is the buried child, the forgotten child, the child interred at night in unconsecrated ground. For some true believers, no doubt, Annie Murphy and her son, her long-buried child, will still be associated with the satanic. Her book will be not just an act of personal betrayal, but an act of sacrilege.

Both of these roles — sheela-na-gig to terrify the Irish church, and desecrator of the faithful's ideas of the sacred — are ones which Annie Murphy is happy to play in her book. They are, after all, starring roles, big parts in a drama that has been played for centuries. To describe making love in the bishop's palace in Killarney, to describe distracting the bishop while he is saying Mass, to mention his cross and ring in the context of furtive coupling, is to be one of the two main players, not in the kitchen tragedy of Annie and Eamonn, but in the grand opera of the clash of eternal forces. It is to play Body to his Soul, avenging angel to his tarnished saint, world, flesh and devil to his Father, Son and Holy Ghost. It is a lot more glorious than to be poor, wounded Annie.

Yet the real story, the story that comes through so painfully in her book once you get used to the strange circumstances of this love affair, is ineffably ordinary. Take away the one sensational aspect of the story — that the man involved is a Catholic bishop, sworn to celibacy and preaching a strict code of sexual morality — and what you are left with is a story that life has told over and over, until it is blue in the face.

A younger, more vulnerable woman meets an older, more powerful man. He dazzles her with his power, his confidence, his command of the world. They fall in love and begin a sexual relationship. He promises her nothing, but he doesn't need to, for hurt and abused as she is, she is more than capable of making him into a promise to herself. She gives him pleasure, excitement and adoration. He gives her the first two but probably not the third. She thinks of the future, he thinks of the present, floating on the delusion that he can have the best of all worlds. He makes her pregnant. The baby forces choices on her, choices which, because he is a man and a powerful one, he doesn't believe he has to make. He behaves badly, hypocritically, politically. It ends in tears: first hers, then, after many years, his.

Take away the thrill of discovering that bishops as a class are no better than many other men, and what remains is the fact that they are no worse. Little would have to change in Annie Murphy's book if Eamonn Casey were a prominent politician, or a judge, or just an ordinary married man indulging in a passionate but doomed side-affair which he will shake off when it becomes too threatening to his marriage and his settled place in the world. Desecration lies in the treacherous, abusive things that people do to each other, not in the fact that they are done in a bishop's palace rather than a bedsit.

We were promised some shocking revelations: that the affair lasted longer than was previously believed and continued after the birth of their son, Peter; that it was conducted for a period in a car parked in a gravel pit in Dublin; that they slept together again in a New York hotel as recently as early 1991. But given the initial premise — that an Irish bishop had an affair and a child — and the inevitable deceptions and moral contortions that flow from it, these are not shocking at all. They come with the territory, and the territory is a well-worn ground of deceit and double-dealing, a landscape that is there whether bishops choose to tread on it or not.

What is actually much more striking in Annie Murphy's story is the shock of the familiar. The view from the bishop's bed is a new angle on the sumptuousness and luxury of life at the top of the clerical ladder. There is nothing shocking in the notion that some bishops live in palaces, eat like kings and behave like princelings, that they are often waited-on, flattered and pampered. But this is seldom described, because outsiders do not get close enough to do so. Annie Murphy is one outsider who did, who became privy to a world whose sensual delights may exclude sex but include the best of food and drink, the finest places to live, the swankiest cars, clothes bought straight from Harrods. She is a privileged reporter, and the value of her testimony lies at least as much in its description of things that are taken for granted by the faithful, as of things that will shock and horrify them.

If there is an extraordinary dimension to this story of ordinary things, it is not the clash of sacred and secular, but the clash of Ireland and Irish-America. Annie Murphy's family could have been invented by Eugene O'Neill, such is its archetypal drama of lace curtain Irish respectability riddled with alcoholism, subdued violence and the hard bitterness of exile. John Steinbeck looked at the Irish-Americans and said that they "do have a despairing gaiety, but they also have a dour and brooding ghost that rides on their shoulders and peers in on their thoughts." Annie Murphy embodies both the despairing gaiety and the brooding ghost, with a view of the world that is often wildly comic and often haunted by nameless forebodings.

Her love for Eamonn Casey seems inextricable from her love for Ireland, an exile's love of the dream homeland. She is in love with the place as much as with the man. The sea, the mountains, the flowers are characters in her love affair. She brings to that affair both the illusory longing and the driven ambition of Irish-America, both the rosy view of Ireland and the all-American drive to make the world conform to her view of it.

In many ways, Eamonn Casey is as typically Irish as she is Irish-American. Energetic, garrulous, at home with the world, but also full of evasions and denials. In certain ways, she is more ambitious than he is, for she wants the world to change, wants a clerical princeling to come down off his throne and take charge of her messy life, while he wants things to be the same only more so. He wants everything he has and something else as well — the joy of sex, maybe the comfort of being loved rather than adored. He just has to make room in his busy life for another pleasure. She has to re-invent the world, make it conform to her desires. It is a clash of mother country and restless exile as much as it is a clash of Mother Church and restless desire.

As in a Greek play, the clash of these incompatible but ineluctable forces can produce only tragedy. The directness which the Irish learned in America cannot communicate with the evasions of life at home. The elaborate cathedral of airy self-justifications which he builds on the restless foundations of his desire is demolished by her impatience. The ambition of her desire, the vision of a future in which she and Eamonn and Peter will live happily ever after, is thwarted by his ability to live with all his contradictions in a never-ending present rather than have to face the hard choices for the future.

The tragedy, strangely, is at its sharpest when the story is most comic. The awful events — the abandonment of a son and the humiliation of an important public man — are awful only because there is a glimmer that things might have been otherwise. What is most wretched about the abandonment of Peter is that there are times when there is another sort of abandonment, times when Annie and Eamonn seem to have abandoned themselves to a kind of exuberant madness in which their laughter mingled into one wild cascade.

There are episodes in their story during which the absurdity of their situation is funny instead of sordid, during which they seem to have been able to stand back and look at themselves and collapse in a helpless laughter.

That kind of removal from oneself, that release into a zone where nothing matters, is what lovers call love and saints call a state of grace. Though the faithful may think it blasphemous, it is neveretheless possible that in those moments of wild laughter, Eamonn Casey and Annie Murphy were in love and in a state of grace at the same time.

If that is so, then it is also possible that the real sacrilege in relation to Annie Murphy's story would be not to allow for those moments when the sacred and the secular, the soul and the body, the monk and the sheela-na-gig, sex and holiness, were, however fleetingly, one and same thing. Because the story is so public, so symbolic, it is easy to overlook this precious intimacy at its core, the sacred humanity without which there would be no tragedy.

Tragedies are supposed to teach us something, and what is to be learned from the tragedy of these hurt people is that a world which insists on neat divisions between the holy and the unholy, between men and women, between courage and hypocrisy, is one which creates tragedies.

Brecht replied to the adage "unhappy the land that has no heroes" with the correction "unhappy the land that needs heroes". Equally, unhappy the Church that needs heroes, that is so threatened and terrified by the revelation that within its upper ranks there exist ordinary human desires and ordinary human hypocrisies. All Annie Murphy has really done is to state the obvious. That she can gain so much notice from doing so is the fault of those who have denied the obvious for too long.

William Butler Yeats stated the obvious more elegantly many years ago in a poem called *Crazy Jane Talks With The Bishop:*

A woman can be proud and stiff

When on love intent;

But Love has pitched his mansion in

The place of excrement;

For nothing can be sole or whole

That has not been rent.

Whether the bishop listened to Crazy Jane or not, Yeats does not tell us. It would be nice to think, though, that some bishops might listen to the strange, abandoned laughter of Annie Murphy and Eamonn Casey before they became hateful and afraid.

A MORALITY DEBATE
GOING NOWHERE

At the begining of last year, The Catholic Archbishop of Dublin, Dr. Desmond Connell, remarked in an interview with the *Sunday Tribune* that homosexuality is "an objective disorder" and therefore represents an "affliction". At the time the remarks created a great deal of offence, seeming as they did, to imply that homosexuality is a disease.

The remark seemed extraordinarily insensitive at best, hopelessly bigoted at worst. In reaction, Professor Anthony Clare in *The Irish Times* set out to show that psychologists do not regard homosexuality as a disorder or a disease, and that Dr. Connell was therefore objectively wrong.

The controversy rumbled for a while and, as such things do, faded into the backround, yet another skirmish in the continuing war between conservative Ireland on the one hand and Liberal Ireland on the other.

What nobody noticed was that this wasn't even a skirmish, never mind a battle. Far from engaging in a confrontation, the two sides had not engaged with each other at all. For what Dr. Connell had seemed to mean in the language of modern scientific reason — that homosexuality is a disease — was not what he meant at all. He was talking quite literally a different language, the language of mediaeval scholastic philosophy drawn from Aristotle and Saint Thomas Aquinas. One of the most powerful men in Ireland, the spiritual leader of a million Catholics, was, in this instance, literally incomprehensible even to his own flock.

If there are such basic problems of comprehension in ordinary areas of debate about issues in Irish society, what chance is there that the continuing wrangles over questions of sexual morality will be anything other than an increasingly sterile war of attrition, a perpetual Somme with both sides wading through the mud to take another few feet of ground, the air thick with impenetrable gases?

The answer, if you read the latest issue of the *Jesuit Quarterly Studies,* may well be very little. In a penetrating but utterly pessimistic essay the Jesuit priest and lecturer at Milltown Institute of Theology and Philosophy, the Rev. Patrick Reardon, asks the question, "Can we not discuss morals?" and comes close to answering "no." Father Reardon argues that "traditional Christian morality is not based on a philosophy equally accessible to believers and non-believers alike" and that this fact "makes the Christian viewpoint so unintelligble in the contemporary world." He concludes from this that, for Catholics, "it is to be expected that our various moral positions will lead to misunderstanding."

This is a bleak view, and it is in fact even bleaker than it seems, for the logic of Father Reardon's argument is not merely that traditional Christian morality is incomprehensible to non-believers, but actually that it is incomprehensible in its fundamental sources to most people in a secularised society, including to ordinary lay Catholics who don't have the benefit of a training in Aristotelian and Tomistic philosophy.

Whatever your views on religion or on the role of the Churches, this is a hugely significant thing to say about a society like Ireland's: that its main source of moral direction for the last 1,500 years has become, by and large, incomprehensible to the society. And remember, this is argued from inside that system of beliefs, not from the outside.

It is worth looking in some detail at this argument, for two basic reasons. One is that until we come to some set of consensus, solutions about issues like contraception, divorce, homosexuality and abortion, these issues, in all their tedium, will continue to dominate our native public life, both in themselves poisoning our democracy

146

(the abortion issue, for instance, has already led to gross acts of censorship like the removal of books on women's health from the public library shelves) and the crowding out of the wider social and economic issues of Ireland and Europe.

The other is that, if you do want to see an open, pluralistic society emerging on this island, then it is vital that the Catholic Church be confident about its place in the world and not embattled to the point of being incommunicado in the way that Father Reardon's analysis implies. The basic idea in traditional Catholic morality is that things must be judged in relation to what they are for, what purpose they are intended to achieve, what point they will end up at, and more importantly, what point they should end up at. The word "order" in the way that Dr. Connell would use it, is inextricably bound up with this way of thinking. There is an order in human relationships, a tendency towards an ideal, which is that of the permanent monogamous nuclear family, and anything which tends in a direction away from this ideal (homosexuality, pre-marital sex, contraception, divorce) is therefore a disorder.

For Dr. Connell to say that homosexuality is a disorder is no more to imply that homosexuality is a disease than the same process of thinking would imply that divorce or using a condom is a disease. Essentially, Catholic moral thinking links order with perfection: the proper order of behaviour is to move towards this perfect ideal.

Modern thinking, on the other hand, works in an utterly different way. It accepts that different people have different ideas of perfection, and that no agreement on what is absolutely and permanently ideal is possible. It looks to build a morality, therefore, on a minimal agreement about what is necessary for people to live together without tyranny.

The classic formulation of this minimal agreement is that of John Stuart Mill: that each of us should be free to do as we wish, provided that our exercise of that freedom doesn't do harm to others. This position, which is at odds with traditional Christian morality and its emphasis on seeking out that goal of perfection, is so firmly established in the modern world that even those who argue for traditional Catholic morality in Ireland actually do so on the basis of Mill's formulation rather that from the ideas of Aristotle and Saint Thomas.

The arguments you are likely to hear against divorce or homosexuality or the availability of condoms, for instance, are all arguments about the supposed harm that these things will do. Even to defenders of traditional Christian morality, the roots of that morality have become incomprehensible.

Is there any way out of this blind alley of argument in which the two sides don't even share a language or a structure of thought and therefore cannot even begin to communicate with each other? Are we doomed to a dialogue of the deaf, which will be resolved only by weight of numbers eventually favouring the liberals or by European leglisation over-riding the lot of us?

It may well be that there is no solution and that real dialogue on these issues is impossible. If that is the case, then we should decide so now, and not waste our time for the next 10 years going through the motions. It is nevertheless the case that each of these systems of morality might have something to learn from the other.

If Catholics can bring that tradition of Christian morality to bear on their society, rather than be content with a bleak reiteration of the incomprehensible into the void, then they have a real moral agenda to offer to a secularised society. And if secular liberals can see that the minimalism of their own morality, which is a morality for tolerable coexistence rather than for changing things for the better, has useful things to learn from the large ambitions of the older tradition, then there are at least grounds for a dialogue. This might well be too much to hope for, but when the alternative is a series of sterile replays of the 1980s referendums, it is a hope worth entertaining.

TERMINATIONS

Contributions To The Abortion Debate
After The X Case

1.

April 1992. The country is riven by the deep divisions opened up by the ruling of the Supreme Court in March, 1992, that a 14-year old girl who had been prevented from leaving the country for an abortion has the right to have her pregnancy terminated.

Last November, I was in Strasbourg for a seminar at the European Parliament. Late in the day, the American novelist William Styron (*The Confessions of Nat Turner, Sophie's Choice*) got up to speak. In contrast to the rotund intensity of the French and Germans, he was easy-going, discursive and optimistic. The question of race, the fearful rise of racism and neo-fascism in Europe, had run like a vein of bad blood through the day's proceedings. Styron offered some hope, speaking movingly and sensibly about the achievements, in spite of everything, of the black rights movement in the United States. As his speech ascended towards its peak, proclaiming "one of the most dramatic reversals of a profound social injustice in history," you could sense, even through the babel of simultaneous translations, that his audience was with him, baroque old Europe refreshed by a breath of the land of opportunity.

Then, Styron veered off and began the descent. He started to speak about abortion, about the way it was, as he put it, tearing American society apart. The debate on abortion in his country, he said, had left "the emotional life of the United States sapped and the intellectual life cheapened and demeaned." As he spoke now, you could sense a weary anger about him, a long-borne private sadness being given a futile public airing. And you could sense, unmistakably, that his audience was now lost. The earphones were taken off one ear, the posture slumped into that peculiar dejection of the long-distance listener. The very notion of a country sapped and cheapened and demeaned by an abortion debate obviously seemed, to these cool Europeans, absurd. Except, of course, if you happened to be Irish.

I thought of that moment again when the King and Queen of Sweden were around last week. Watching their perfectly polished poise, their sense of representing a finished and self-confident society, I couldn't help wondering what they thought about being dragged into our little traumas. Did they know that they (or rather what they represented) had been pulled and dragged at for our own purposes? That there were people hoping they wouldn't come, and so deliver a message of European shock to our naïve cruelties? That there were sermons being preached about them in the parish churches of Ireland? Did they hear about the priest's sermon in the west of Ireland a few weeks back: "We are reminded that the Swedish parliament advised their king and queen not to proceed with a proposed diplomatic visit to Ireland. That is their prerogative, but that same Sweden isn't behind the door when it comes to supplying arms to terrorist groups throughout the world." Could they have begun to understand for one moment why a man of the cloth in the West of Ireland felt it so necessary to slander their country in this bizarre way, why, as Styron put it, the intellectual life of a nation gets so cheapened and demeaned when the subject for debate is abortion?

Nor is the obsession with abortion which rends our society shared even in the rest of the Catholic world. In Britain, for instance, SPUC felt the need to lambaste the Catholic bishops of England and Wales for making no more than "the most meaningless reference" to abortion in their checklist of questions for election candidates. In Italy last month the Catholic Archbishop of Bologna, Cardinal Biffi, denounced as "foreign fanatics" demonstrators, including a Scottish priest, who blocked a corridor in an abortion clinic.

Maybe it's worth considering for a moment why it is that Ireland and the United States are so riven by the abortion debate, while other western societies which share our basic white Christian civilisation aren't. Obviously, the two societies are immensely different, but there are two reasons for looking at them together in relation to this issue. One is that there are real and immediate connections (from the American priests who started the ball rolling here to the legal precedent of Roe v. Wade). The other is that anything that might help to lift the claustrophobia of our present morass by looking to a wider context is worthwhile.

What might be said of both Ireland and the United States is that they are countries with a sense of frustrated destiny. Both share the contradiction that they have had more utopian ideas about themselves than other western societies, yet they have had less utopian politics. Whereas most western societies injected utopian ideas (either Christian or socialist or both) into their politics and then successfully domesticated them into the standard Christian Democrat/Social Democrat dichotomy, Ireland and America, for different reasons, kept their utopias pure of politics. The Americans had Manifest Destiny, or, later, the empire of light that stood against the evil empire of communism, notions which while never apolitical were mostly supra-political. The Irish had a mystically conceived united Ireland which would act as a last bastion of Holy Europe, a moral beacon to the world. In neither case were these big notions ever fully domesticated into ordinary party politics.

Now, with the collapse of utopias and big projects, most western societies have been able to cope quite comfortably because their utopias were already nicely house-broken and harmless. This is untrue of either Ireland or America.

The Americans have had it hard: achieving an unthinkable utopian dream— winning the Cold War— and finding that it makes no difference. The Irish, though, have had it tough as well. Even unreconstructed Ireland knows in its heart that the utopian games are up, that Ireland will only be united when that, too, makes no difference, and that the kindling for our beacon has been irreparably dampened by the hard rain of reality. For both societies, or at least for those within them who cannot live without a sense of destiny, there is just one utopia left, the most primitive and powerful of all: the womb.

Our image of the womb as the ultimate harbour of safety and innocence is, we need to be reminded, not a universal or a historic one. It is in fact the very opposite of the popular image of a few hundred years ago in Europe, which still survives in many parts of the world. The belief that pregnant women were bad magic because of the capriciousness of the child in the womb who could cause crops to be blighted or the hunt to fail had its counterpart in quite recent popular Catholicism in the refusal of communion to menstruating women or the churching of women who had given birth. For much of the history of Catholic ritual, the ceremony of baptism was combined with an exorcism, on the grounds that the child emerging from the womb had been in a dangerous place, vulnerable to possession by the devil. It is only as belief in other forms of utopia, other magical transformations, has declined, that our notion of the womb as the perfect, pure place has developed.

And a wonderful notion it is, that state of pure possibility in which nothing has yet been compromised or lost, in which no choices have to be made, in which we do not have to struggle for our needs to be fulfilled, in which there is no painful memory and no tormenting desire. There is nothing odd or contemptible about the way in which societies like Ireland or America, nations which have a haunting sense of having taken a wrong turning, of

153

having wandered inadvertently from the path of their destiny into dense undergrowth, become fascinated with the idea of a return to the point of origin, with the desire to wind back the clock and return to a primal state of pure possibility. Going back to the womb is a lot more attractive than slogging on through the brambles.

Yet, the lesson of this century is that utopias can quickly turn into the tyranny of those who believe in them. That lesson has to be learned in Ireland now. We have to learn that utopias function properly as ideas and as images, not as laws and regimes. We also have to learn that the wrench away from the womb and its innocence, into the harsh lights of choice and loss, is a precondition for growth. Whatever about Life, we know that our lives begin with that moment of shock and chill. We take it, as we have to, from there.

2.

August 1992. The country is transfixed by two events. In Barcelona, Michael Carruth wins a gold medal in the Olympic boxing tournament. Meanwhile a baby missing in England is found in the home of a young Clare woman.

In the last ten days, two dramatically contrasting images of the Irish family have dominated public consciousness. One was the image of a boundless presence, the other of an aching absence. In one image, that of the Carruth household in Dublin, there was an almost exaggeratedly bountiful image of the Irish family: triplets, infants, brothers, sisters, a wonderful mother, an archetypal father, all overflowing from the television screen in joy and warmth. In the other, there was a hollow voice from a house in Clare saying "Go away" through the letterbox, a faceless anonymous young woman projected through her pain into the tabloid headlines, driven to a desperate act by the haunting absence of her lost twins. It was as if one image needed to be corrected by the other, as if, in learning to grapple with the dark intimacies of Irish life, we have to be taught to embrace and understand and identify with both of these images together.

Sometimes, when it looks into the heart of a private grief, Ireland can muster a spirit of kindness, temperance and tact that makes up for so much else. In the euphoria which followed the return of their daughter Farrah, Bernadette and Shane Quli expressed the happiness that they felt on learning that their missing baby was being sought in Ireland. In the midst of such a nightmare, all the sentimental hypocrisy about the loveliness of our land is redeemed by the knowledge that the word "Ireland" can still bring such comfort to the distressed.

And, from the other side of the story, there was something moving about the compassion which the Gardai involved in the case obviously felt for the young woman from whose home the baby was rescued. A woman who had been set up for demonisation suddenly, when she became real, when she was placed amidst the rooted anguish of recognisable humanity, attracted nothing but tenderness and sympathy.

Yet the obverse of this reassuring story is that it takes such extremes of drama to awaken the latent sense of the complexity and difficulty which surround issues of birth and motherhood which most Irish people have. The nice aspect of the Baby Farrah story, the refusal to see it as a simple morality tale with a good mother on the one side and a wicked witch on the other, is one which is too seldom present when we touch on these most sensitive of areas.

George Bernard Shaw asked "Must a Christ be crucified in every generation in order to save those without imagination?" We might also ask whether a Baby Farrah must be abducted every year in order to save from the grim simplicities about motherhood those who do not have the imagination to understand the destructive power of simplicity.

What the Qulis and the Gardai and most Irish people were struck by, even in the joy of a happy ending, was the pain of the young woman from whose house the baby was rescued. Nobody agreed with what she had done. Nobody was unmoved by the joy of the reunion of Farrah with her parents. But precisely because there was no argument, no balancing of rights and wrongs, the sympathy for that young woman could be of a pure kind. Repulsion at the act clarified rather than muddied the sense of her grief and anguish and need.

When that kind of sympathy is engaged in a particular case, Irish people emerge as peculiarly compassionate and non-judgemental. Yet, the compassion that we can muster in the concrete case is still extremely difficult for us to manage in the abstract. There are very few people in Ireland who would want that woman punished, who would want the crude mechanism of the law put into motion to deal with her desperation. If asked to enunciate principles which should govern the approach to a case like this, I imagine that most people, of whatever background or religious persuasion, would say that the first rule must be sympathy, an open understanding of the actual circumstances of life in which people can find themselves. I think that most people would want a way of dealing with such things which recognises that the blind operation of the law is not the only locus of morality, that there are more things in the heart of man and woman than can be dreamt of in jurisprudence or criminology.

And the point is that we respond like this to this sort of case not because we are careless of the importance of parenthood and children, but because we care so much about these things. Precisely because there is such a strong place in the culture for children and childbearing, there can also be a compassionate understanding of the tragic needs that might drive a woman to take someone else's child. Out of the very basis of a supposedly conservative ethic — the much-abused "family values" — we can make

156

something that is morally complex and expansive rather than something narrow and rigid.

We can use our imaginations to get a sense of what the woman in Toni Morrison's wonderful novel *Jazz* feels when she contemplates stealing a baby: "When the baby was in her arms, she inched its blanket up around the cheeks against the threat of wind too cool for its honey-sweet, butter-coloured face. Its big-eyed non-committal stare made her smile. Comfort settled itself in her stomach and a kind of skipping, running light travelled her veins." But the hard task is to turn that familial imagination, which makes us admirable, into an idea of law and morality that can survive its removal from the particular and concrete humanity of one woman into our constitution and laws. Is it possible that we could build a structure of legality that does justice both to our "family values" and to our compassionate imagination, both to our ideals and to our sympathies?

In order to be able to do so, we need to start by valuing motherhood more not less. At present, we both idealise it and devalue it, sending out confused signals that add greatly to the suffering involved when things go wrong. We carry around sacred images of the Virgin Mother and of the foetus in the womb, making them into holy symbols to be brandished in the faces of the godless. But we equally easily make light of the actual process of motherhood. The emotional appeals to the girl in the X case to simply have her baby and give it up for adoption, implied that such a course of action might be relatively easy, a small sacrifice to make. The momentary glimpse into the anguish of a woman who did have to give her children up for adoption which we have had in the last few days should be a reminder of the pain and difficulty that can surround any option — adoption, keeping the baby, abortion — which a woman in the midst or the aftermath of a crisis pregnancy might consider. The mixture of idealisation and devaluation which surrounds motherhood has kept out of

157

our public culture the sheer difficulty involved in even the happiest of pregnancies. We present motherhood as a fixed and timeless ideal, yet experience it as a realm in which there are no easy options, in which any joy is hard-won, in which no fixed pattern holds and every moment of decision must be faced anew and more or less alone.

Only when the silent struggles that surround every aspect of child-bearing all the time fail spectacularly, only when a girl dies giving birth alone or a young woman steals a baby out of grief and need, do we allow the secret knowledge of that difficulty to manifest itself in a sympathy that recognises a common area of experience. Such dramatic events allow us to be at our best: modest, tolerant and unself-righteous. By being sufficiently humble about ourselves to recognise our kinship with a woman who has done a terrible thing, we also do ourslves proud. It would be good, entering as we are into a period of intense debate about family, pregnancy and childbirth in Ireland, to move forward in this spirit, staking our pride, not on our supposed ability to be a beacon of righteousness to the rest of the world, but on the humility with which we can recognise the real anguish of real people.

3.

October, 1992. The Irish government issues its proposals for dealing with the constitutional issues involved in the X case, and proposes to allow abortion only where necessary to protect the "life but not the health" of the mother.

"Ah, solving that question," wrote Philip Larkin

Brings the priest and the doctor

In their long coats

Running over the fields.

You can already hear their coat-tails flapping in the breeze as they come bounding over a jagged landscape of cynicism and confusion, towards a hospital bed where a pregnant woman lies in pain and fear. And, from behind them, you can just hear the approach of an army of lawyers bustling up the hill, holding their wigs on with one hand and swinging constitutional tomes in the other. If it were a picture, it would be one of those grotesque Hogarth engravings of an anatomy lesson, middle-aged men in wigs and mortar boards prodding and poking at a cadaver that is stretched on a table in an ill-lit room. Except for an added refinement of the horror: the body is not a cadaver, but a living, pregnant woman.

There is another characteristic sound of the pronouncements on abortion in the last few days. It is the sound of air bubbles breaking the surface, of waves gently lapping over balding heads, of flailing arms thrashing the waters. It is the sound of men who have wandered in past their depth, wearing the hob-nailed boots of political expediency that make them now too clumsy and heavy to turn around and come back again. Men who can't deal with the things that are supposed to be their business, like jobs and houses and hospitals, suddenly decided that they were up to dealing with nothing less than Life and Death. They discovered their hidden depths and plunged straight into them.

If it is deeply problematic even for people with a clear and well thought-out knowledge of a difficult moral area to make decisions which are binding on other peoples' consciences, it borders on obscenity for people who do not know what they themselves think to presume to take command of other peoples' lives. Since almost all of the people who are doing the proclaiming are men, and all those whose lives are put at risk by their chaotic self-righteousness are women, the offence is all the greater. What we now have is a situation in which womens' lives are to be put at risk, in which their despair is to be dismissed, for the sake of a principle which even those who want to enforce it are utterly unclear about.

Like the Sorcerer's Apprentice, our Government has put on the magician's hat and called up the fundamental forces of human life and human death. It has muttered spells in a language it doesn't understand, commanding these forces to wash out its kitchen. And now, it is up to its neck in water. A litany of the confusions and contradictions which it has already thrown up in a few days of discussion would take up most of this page. But two representative samples give good grounds for believing that it has only the vaguest idea of what it is talking about.

Take firstly the simplest of questions, one that doesn't even involve the complexities of what effect the Government's proposed wording will have. In a quiz show this would be the easy starter: was abortion legal in Ireland before the Supreme Court ruling in the X case? Mr Reynolds says it wasn't. His Attorney General says it was. Last Friday, Mr Reynolds told the Dail that the X case ruling had "legalised abortion in certain circumstances in this country... that is not acceptable to the Government." Fine. But counsel for the Attorney General told the Supreme Court before the X case ruling that abortion was already legal in Ireland under the 1983 amendement.

Then take the more complex question of "direct" and "indirect" abortion. Over the weekend we got a barrage of warnings from the Government not to use these terms, since they have no legal or medical standing. First a Government spokesman, then Mr Padraig Flynn and then Mr Reynolds told us over the weekend that these terms were irrelevant and confusing. Again, fine. It is true that these terms have no place either in medicine or in law, that it is a legal and moral absurdity to suppose that you do not intend to take responsibility for all of the foreseeable consequences of your actions. So Mr Reynolds was right to warn us on Sunday that these were "not the words that should be used by anybody".

But the people who had been using them were not just anybody, but Mr Reynolds, the Attorney General and the

Minister for Health, Dr John O'Connell, and the Government Press Secretary. Four senior figures, including the Taoiseach himself, have been using the words — and the concepts behind them — that they now say are irrelevant, confusing and not to be used by anybody.

Mr Reynolds used them on Thursday when he told us that "the fundamental principle was opposition to direct intervention to kill a foetus." The fundamental principle, mind you, yet one which can be abandoned and become unusable by Sunday evening. The Attorney General used them in the briefing document which is supposedly the basis for the Government's decisions. Dr O'Connell used them on RTE on Thursday night, telling us that "aggressive treatment of a woman to save her life may amount to direct abortion. So, we are saying, indirect abortion." And, on Friday, in what was laughably called a "clarification" a Government spokesman said that "direct abortion" would not be permitted "even if it's to save the life of the mother."

Yet, it gets worse. For not alone did the Government abandon its "fundamental principle" in a matter of days, it couldn't even be sure whether it had abandoned it or not. In the very same statement in which the Government spokesman gave us the new line — that "direct" and "indirect" were confusing terms without legal or medical basis — he continued to use the concept that lies behind them. "What we are trying to convey," he told us, is that a woman can be assured of "whatever treatment is necessary, even if that results in the unintentional loss of the foetus." But "unintentional" in this context is a direct synonym for "indirect." The terms are interchangeable. It depends on the same legal fallacy — that the consequences of a medical intervention are unintentional even though they are known about precisely in advance. So the Government continues to use terms which it itself tells us are confusing and have no legal or medical basis.

The breathtaking gall of these people only really becomes clear, however, when you consider that they then assume the right to question the credibility of a girl or a woman in extreme distress who threatens suicide. They, whose own confusion is such that they can contradict their own "fundamental principles" virtually from day to day, who have become utterly incredible in their capacity for shifting between opposites, believe that they can blithely dismiss the credibility of desperate people in desperate situations.

Their wording rules out the "risk of self-destruction" as a criterion for abortion. The Taoiseach has told us that this is because the threat of suicide is an easy one to make. Easier, I wonder, than finding a "fundamental principle" and sticking to it? Easier than using the English language with some kind of clarity and consistency? Easier than working out what you believe before you proffer it as an imposition on other people?

But the arrogance of people whose credibility has been destroyed by self-contradiction passing a dismissive judgement on the credibility of others should not blind us to the chilling implications of this dismissal. If a girl who is raped and is pregnant is not to be believed when she says she will kill herself, why should she be believed when she says she was raped? Is it easier to threaten to kill yourself than it is to go through a rape trial? Apparently the Government believes it is. Apparently it also believes that girls or women in these circumstances will say anything that comes into their head. How can a woman who is not to be believed when the life of a month-old foetus is at stake, be believed when the potential life imprisonment of her attacker is at stake? It is, presumably, an easy accusation to make.

In all the confusion only one thing is clear: that we have a Government with a chillingly reductive view of life. The new concept of life-as-distinct-from-health amounts to saying "never mind the quality, feel the pulse." Life means merely not being dead. It is Star Trek morality, a case of "It's life, Padraig, but not as we know it." Beam us up, Scotty.

4.

OCTOBER 1992. The debate continues.

"There was a priest there a long time ago," begins the folktale from Kerry collected by Anne O'Connor, "and there used be spirits going around at that time." The priest was coming home from anointing a dying man, and he came to a river. A woman stood there before him. She jumped up behind him on his horse. He took out his stole and tied her to him. She asked him to release her and he said "I won't, you proper hussy." He tried to bring her into the first two houses they came to, but she couldn't go in, because they were houses where the Rosary was said. Finally, they came to a house which she could enter and he forced her on her two knees in the middle of the floor.

"What damned you, you harlot?" he asked.

"I killed a man," said she.

"That didn't damn you, you devil," said the priest.

"I killed a woman,"said she.

"That didn't damn you," said the priest.

"I killed a child," said she, "to save its mother, an unbaptised child."

"That's what damned you, you devil," said he.

The priest read a bit from his Bible over her and "put her into the Red Sea, a place from which she will not be going about killing the people, a place in which she will be till the end of the world."

Such stories were found in many parts of the country up to the late 1960s, stories in which the midwife who committed the awful crime of saving the mother rather than the baby is banished forever by a fearless priest. Child-killing women — Petticoat Loose, Máire Gaelach,

163

Marta Scot and other names — literally haunt the landscape, lying in wait for unsuspecting travellers, doomed to wander as pariahs until they are exorcised and cast into exterior darkness.

The unbaptised babies also lay in wait. To walk across the burial place was to be stricken with hunger, or to be lead astray, or to be stricken with a skin rash. Even in the 1940s, a folklorist was able to get the following explanation as to why you would lose your way if you walked over the grave of an unbaptised infant: "An unbaptised child is in darkness, and will continue so until the Day of Judgement, and when a person treads on the spot, where that child is buried, he walks into the darkness, he is surrounded by it, and consequently, he goes astray."

This world of darkness and devils, of the living dead, of fears and hatreds that were physically present in our fields and roads and rivers is gone. It is not as distant as we like to think — I lived for the first 20 years of my life in a Dublin suburb with a grandfather who still believed in these things — but nowadays different things fill our darkest imaginings. What I wonder, though, is whether the fears and hatreds which the old stories gave breath to are also gone. Or do we just find new images, new myths, for them?

What the old stories and superstitions remind us of is that there is nothing new in our torments over pariah-women and unborn babies. These questions haunted our mental and physical landscapes long before we had constitutions, never mind constitutional amendments. Then, as now, it was possible to walk across the secret burial places and be enveloped in darkness.

The world we live in now is one of movies and Madonna, of satellites and scandals. The only ghostly images we discern are when there is something wrong with the television reception. If a dark and terrifying figure appears on a country lane, she is probably an inspector of taxes. We still have spirits that waylay us, but they are beamed at us from outer space. Yet it may be that they still have the same power to give form and shape to fears that are no less primal and deeply-rooted for being expressed in the language of Hollywood.

I am thinking of an extraordinarily tangled set of images let loose by the anti-abortion consultant, Dr Louis Courtney, on *Questions and Answers* the other night. Dr Courtney is interesting because his patent sincerity and passion have not yet been processed into well-groomed television etiquette. Unlike most people on all sides of the debate who speak their lines, he speaks his mind. He gives a glimpse into his thought-process. And it this thought-process rather than its result — a familiar anti-abortion position — that is most striking.

He began to ponder the word "terminate," as in "It shall be unlawful to terminate the life of an unborn unless such temination is necessary..." It became clear that the word itself upset him deeply. He could not see it in terms other than those of a particularly violent movie. Talking about the medical practice of trying to save both mother and baby, he said, "We didn't terminate the baby. We didn't pull off its head."

And he did, in fact, locate this image in a half-remembered set of movie moments. He said that there was a film called *The Terminator*. The terminator in question, he went on, "apparently had an Irish accent." He went around killing people from a distance. What he was thinking of, apparently, was Arnold Schwarzenegger in *The Terminator* movies, which are, indeed, modern folklore. Since, however, Mr Schwarzenegger, who is Austrian, is not noted for his Irish accent, and since he likes to kill people close up rather than from a distance, I can only guess that Dr Courtney may have been thinking of Marlon Brando in *The Missouri Breaks*, where he plays an Irish-accented killer who likes to pick off his victims from a great distance.

Whatever about that, the interesting thing is the revelation of this mythic incarnation of evil, lurking in the head of a sincere opponent of abortion in any circumstances, a highly educated and highly intelligent late-20th century professional man. He would seem to have constructed for himself, from the modern mythology of Hollywood movies, a vision of a creature with an Irish accent who goes around pulling the heads off babies. This vision is for our world what the satanic midwives and baby-killers of our greatgrandparents' imaginations were to theirs. It has the power to haunt a late-20th century imagination in precisely the way that the wicked midwives haunted the fields and roads and churchyards of an older time.

We know what the old world's fears were about: things that were neither one thing nor the other. The wicked women were neither dead nor alive, because they had committed the sin of trying to take control of life and death. The unbaptised babies were halfway between this world and the next, dead but unable to enter heaven. They were buried in places that were regarded as dividing lines between this world and the other world: old monastic sites, ancient stone monuments, lone bushes, boundaries. Like all relatively simple cultures, ours was terrified of things that could not be defined as one thing or the other.

The wicked women and the dangerous babies were banished, not just by electric lights and cars and televisions, but by the development of a moral imagination rather than a mythic one. We learned not to be so afraid of things that were neither one thing nor the other, but in between. But as this process gathered pace, as we became in so many ways a "both/and" society rather than an "either/or" society, the fear, for some of us, returned. New images of evil, clothed in Hollywood costume rather than in the garish colours of superstition, came back to haunt us. We began to insist that women and babies be seen in terms of stark choices of good and evil rather than as people who sometimes exist in those dark zones of uncertainty that terrify those whose moral imagination cannot cope with undefined things.

Just as the old images of fear were banished by an acceptance of moral complexity, so too must the new ones be. The only answer to those fears is a rigorous acceptance of the fact that there are times when the rigid distinctions between life and death, between good and bad, are inadequate. Instead of providing that answer, the Government is pressing ahead with an attempt to solve the problem and calm the fears by adding yet further rigid distinctions — between life and health, between a mental threat to life and a physical one. They are offering a mock-certainty as a substitute for the old certainties. By doing so, they are ensuring that whatever happens in the referendum, the evil spirits, whether from folklore or from Hollywood, will continue to haunt this country.

In the referendum, the Irish people voted to amend the Constitution to secure the right to information on abortion and the right to travel. The Government's proposals to defend the "life but not the health" of mothers were heavily defeated.

THE IRISH FAMILY

It has often seemed to me that the reason we in Ireland have retained a ban on divorce long after most developed societies got rid of theirs is not because the nuclear family is so strong here, but because it is so weak. We have this notion in our heads that marriage and the family are somehow more sacred to us than to other, more benighted nations. It is a deep untruth, an inaccuracy so grotesque that only the might and authority of the Constitution can conceal it. We use a formula of words in our most sacred document of nationhood to assuage a real pain, to calm a chaos in our lives. The nuclear family — Mammy, Daddy and the kids, and they alone, living in one house — is a recent social invention, a product of industrial society. Societies that industrialised in the 19th century also developed the nuclear family as a norm. By the middle of the 20th century, they were beginning to grapple with the limits and failures that this new model produced. In a way, divorce legislation was a kind of backhanded compliment to the nuclear family, now so strongly established that any opting out had to be regulated and legislated for. Here, though, because we developed the nuclear family as the norm so late, and because its hold has been in many ways so tenuous, we are only now beginning to face its failures.

We tend to forget that when, for instance, my parents married in 1955, they were doing something that was more unusual in Ireland than anywhere else in the world. At that time, 64 per cent of the Irish population was single, 6 per cent widowed, and only 30 per cent married. An analysis by Roy Geary of the 1946 census showed that of males in the 15 to 29 age-group, 92 per cent were unmarried. Even in the 20 to 39 age-group, 72 per cent of men were bachelors. When you take account of the high number of priests and the unknown number of homosexuals, this was utterly extraordinary. In the USA at the same time, for instance, half the men were married at 24 and half the women at 21.

Nor was the typical Irish family what conservatives now mean by The Family. For one thing, contrary to the myth, women did not necessarily work in the home. In 1986, the proportion of women engaged in home duties (53.4 per cent) was larger than the proportion in 1936 (51.5 per cent). All the nonsense about social breakdown being due to women not staying at home as they did in the good old days is based on fantasy, not fact.

For another, contrary to the Constitution's insistence on the family as the fundamental unit group of society, the avoidance of families was much more fundamental to the nature of 20th century Ireland up to the 1960s. As the economist James Meenan put it in the 1960s "the society that emerged from the later decades of the 19th century was largely based on the refusal of many of its members of the opportunity to found a home and family. In demographic terms, this was an evil quite as harmful as emigration; in human terms it was more monstrous by far."

And, of course, emigration itself, then as now, was the great wrecker of families. It divided children from their parents, and often also divided husbands and wives in a pattern of family life not far removed from that of South African hostel dwellers.

We really only took to the nuclear family in a big way when we underwent our own industrial revolution in the late 1950s and into the 1960s. Because of all the blather about traditions, it is easy to forget that what we have been through in relation to the family is, to say the least, highly unusual. As Finola Kennedy puts it in the ESRI research paper *Family Economy and Government in Ireland*: "The Irish case may well be unique in the history of family studies. Within the space of a single generation — from the 1950s to the 1980s — the patterns of the traditional extended family dissolved and were replaced by the norm of the nuclear unit." The reason for reminding ourselves of all of this in the wake of last week's Supreme Court judgement and the beginnings of a new divorce debate is that the last debate was won by people who argued that there was such as The Irish Family that it was our duty to "preserve". Before getting back into all that rhetoric, we need to remember that what we now think of as the typical Irish family is a very recent phenomenon, forged, not by tradition, but by extraordinarily rapid, and in some respects traumatic, social change. The family protected by de Valera's Constitution is a family we would now find it hard to recognise — a family based on very late marriage, massive rates of non-marriage, an understanding of children as economic investments and a whole range of kinship allegiances typical of a rural society. Far from being capable of preservation, it is already long gone and, for the most part, it is a good riddance. What we have to do as a society is to acknowledge that we have invented a new kind of Irish family life and try to find legal and social structures that reflect it. In trying to do this, we have to start from a recognition that there is a real relationship between economics and the family, a much more profound one than that implied in the 1986 slogan "Divorce impoverishes women and children — Vote No." Just as the kind of families we now regard as the norm are a product of economic change, so too many (though of course by no means all) of the problems which families encounter are also a result of economic change. Unemployment, the creation of dependency cultures in working-class areas, emigration — these are all central aspects of family breakdown, and they cannot honestly be left out of the debate.

Secondly, we must also start from the recognition that we already have divorce in Ireland. What we do not have is re-marriage. The 1991 census shows 55,143 adults describing themselves as separated from their spouses, an increase of nearly 50 per cent on the figures at the time of the last divorce referendum. The defeat of that proposed constitutional amendment, to put it mildly, did nothing to preserve the Irish family. The undesirable consequences of marital breakdown — the trauma for children, and the poverty of separated women — are already with us, regardless of whether we vote to allow the right of re-marriage to separated people. Indeed, the only effect of denying the right of re-marriage is to deny separated women one of the more obvious routes out of poverty — marrying someone else.

The stark fact is that the biggest single risk of poverty in Ireland, apart from unemployment, is having children. As Combat Poverty studies have consistently shown, households with large numbers of children are increasingly likely to fall into poverty. If the object of State family policy is to be the prevention of poverty, as implied in most anti-divorce argument, then a far more effective mechanism for achieving this aim would be to introduce a Constitutional prohibition on having more than three children, a measure that is probably unlikely to find favour with Family Solidarity, or, indeed, with anyone else. Yet it is as sensible — or as daft — as believing that the way to combat family poverty is to maintain a constitutional prohibition on re-marriage.

Irish Times, February 1994

Politics

SCENES FROM THE DEATH OF THE NATIONAL MOVEMENT

Gradually, over the course of the first two years of the 1990s, the old Fianna Fáil died. The party remained in power, but its nature altered fundamentally, with the loss of the Presidential election in 1990, the ousting of Charles Haughey, his replacement by Albert Reynolds, the disastrous election campaign of 1992 and finally the formation of a "partnership" Government with Labour, abandoning forever Fianna Fáil's claim to be more than just another political party. These events were not just a part of the cycle of politics. They were also the death-throes of a whole conception of Ireland in politics. The party that had invented, sustained and enforced the idea of "Ireland" as a political space finally had to admit that, like everybody else, it was whistling in the dark.

1.

October 1990. In the course of the Presidential election campaign, Brian Lenihan, the Fianna Fáil candidate, denies ever having made phone calls to the incumbent Patrick Hillery, in 1982 urging him not to dissolve the Dail. A research student produces a tape of an interview with Lenihan in which he spoke of having made such a call.

"This is an operative statement. The others are inoperative." Thus Richard Ziegler, Richard Nixon's press

173

secretary, explained that previous statements about Nixon's involvement in Watergate were untrue. In the world of inoperative statements, language becomes a hall of mirrors, forever throwing back a distorted reflection of itself, the relationship to reality becoming weirder and weirder.

The more Brian Lenihan says "my position is perfectly clear," the more you know the opposite is the case. Once begun, a little lie takes on a life of its own, becoming a fast breeder reactor of radioactive language. We all know the feeling: you take a harmless turn off the road of reality and there you are in a maze of falsehoods. You get in so far that there is no going back.

The Lenihan lies have this quality of almost complete purity about them. Usually, with political lies, there is a truth out there somewhere, waiting to be discovered, and the lie is merely the opposite of the truth. But here, the lie is a free-floating entity. It is not an attempt to cover-up something which is patently shameful in the way that, say, Nixon's lies were. And, even more extraordinarily, there is no accepted truth in the matter.

It is quite possible that both versions of what did or did not happen are untrue. The whole thing is entirely self-enclosed: Brian Lenihan playing the role both of accuser and accused, his own disembodied voice on the tape contradicting his own disembodied voice on the television. It is a story out of Kafka or Beckett, not one out of Agatha Christie or Raymond Chandler. All statements are inoperative.

It takes a lot of practice to achieve this kind of pure, free-floating perfection. The thing we're supposed to notice about the whole affair is how sadly ironic it is that the great verbal escape artist has been caught, how strange it is that the slipperiest of eels should have been enmeshed in a verbal net of his own devising. But the point, surely, is the opposite: that the lie is merely plamás raised to the nth degree, that before you can construct this sort of lie for its own sake you have to already have constructed a sort of language for its own sake. You need free floating words, words so completely divorced from reality that they constitute a fact-free zone, in order to be able to utter this sort of completely unreal lie.

Perhaps it begins with de Valera and the signing of the oath, with words as "an empty political formula ... nothing more than an empty formula ... an empty formality."

Certainly it continues with all that de facto and de jure stuff in which reality is recognised as only conditionally real, real on sufferance. Words already begin to take on a life of their own, already start to be spoken in ready made quotation marks.

Certainly, it reaches some sort of zenith in the last decade. In his *Ireland 1912-1985*, Professor Joe Lee describes Brian Lenihan as "an amicable virtuoso of shadow language", and there have been ample opportunities for the display of virtuosity. In the shadow language, words mean what the speaker wants them to mean and, as in Lewis Carroll, whatever I tell you three times is true.

Who could forget Brian Lenihan's claim, after Mr. Haughey's "totality of relationships" meeting with Mrs. Thatcher, that "institutional structures" were the same as constitutional structures, that everything was on the table, that we were within a few years of achieving something which would satisfy our aspirations towards a united Ireland? Who can forget the fun we all had some time later with the insistence of Messrs. Haughey and Lenihan that their statement that constitutional change in Northern Ireland would "come about only" by the consent of the majority was radically different from Garret FitzGerald's statement that constitutional change in Northern Ireland would "require" the consent of the majority?

Who can forget the awfulness of the Anglo-Irish Agreement or the dangers of the Single European Act?

Who can forget the definition of young Irish emigrants as "part of a global generation of Irish people"? We may not all be able to live on a small island, but those of us who do sure can have larks with language.

None of this bothered us too much. "In the big lie," as Adolf Hitler, who knew a bit about the subject put it, "there is always a certain force of credibility ... In the primitive simplicity of their minds, the great masses of the people more readily fall victim to the big lie than to the small lie." In the primitive simplicity of our minds, the lies on the billboards, up in the big letters like "Health cuts hurt the old, the sick and the handicapped" have a certain force of credibility because we take them to be a promise rather than a warning of what is to come.

In the economy of truth, inflation is rampant, and the bigger the lie gets, the harder it is to be outraged. We can wrap our minds around a little lie like Brian Lenihan's but not around the bigger ones which created the language for it. We forget that it is not for nothing that Brian Lenihan's "mature recollection and full reflection" is strikingly reminiscent of de Valera's looking into his own heart. In both, you discover the truth by a process of pure introspection, without recourse to any outside evidence. What begins as a sort of well-meaning mysticism ends up as a sad exercise in mystification.

If it is really only the little lies that we can get worked up about, then it is all the more important that we get worked up about them, since they are tokens of the bigger ones. They are the tip of an iceberg of frozen meanings, empty formulae, dead rhetoric, words designed to obscure rather than elucidate, to mislead rather than to point us in the right direction. If we want to avoid the iceberg, we have to keep away from the tip. It would be nice if, at the end of this affair, we could echo the words of Vaclav Havel:

"The stifling pall of hollow words that have smothered us for so long has cultivated in us such a deep distrust of the world of deceptive words that we are now better equipped than ever before to see the human world as it really is."

"How easy it is," Havel has written, "for a well-intentioned cause to be transformed into the betrayal of its own good intentions — and yet again because of a word whose meaning does not seem to have been kept under adequate observation. Something like that can happen so easily that it almost takes you unawares: it happens inconspicuously, quietly, by stealth — and when at last you realise it, there is only one option left to you: belated astonishment."

Now that we have exercised our option of belated astonishment at what can happen to words in our public life, we should not so easily be caught unawares again.

2.

Autumn 1991. A rash of scandals hits the Government, involving public companies and transactions, including events in Greencore, Telecom Eireann, and the purchase of Carysfort College.

About thirty years ago a group of highly-placed public sector managers, private chartered accountants and business people met in Jury's hotel in Dublin in order to receive gifts from a professor of Commerce. Over bacon and eggs and sausages — then called "high tea" — these self made men, buddies of long standing, congratulated each other on how well they had done in life and anticipated the reward of their station. Among the accountants and money men were the heads of a number of semi-state bodies: the general manager of Aer Lingus, the managing director of the Industrial Credit Corporation and the Chairman of CIE. They were a cabal of allies who had met at UCD, come up through Fianna Fáil and the rise to power of a new generation in a new state and had maintained a network of contacts throughout their career. And now it was time for the pay-off. The professor took it

177

from his bag as the meal finished and put it in the centre of the table. The managers and money men thrust their hands into it and divided it up. It was a large box of sweets.

The wide-eyed innocence of this incident, recounted in his autobiography by one of those present, Todd Andrews, had about it an air of the ludicrous, even then. But that ludicrous innocence of an old professor rewarding his most successful students with a big box of sweets is a lot less disconcerting than the bitter cynicism which a citizen of this state witnessing such a meeting in one of our finer hotels would be forced into nowadays. And there was a kind of truth behind the innocence. Todd Andrews could reasonably, after a life of power and immersion in business and finance on behalf of his country, call his autobiography *Man of No Property*.

In that book, Andrews looked back on the generation of people, of whom he was one, who came to the fore in the building of the state, the privileged new elite who came to lead the public sector. "We had joined Bridge Clubs. We had sampled alcohol and eaten out in restaurants. Some of us had developed views on wine and how to cook steak. We had even modified our views on cosmetics and womens' dress. We had visited France. . . Our surrender to the bourgeois way of life might be measured by the readiness of our acceptance of its trappings. . . In fairness it should be said that none of us ever got grandiose notions about ourselves or about our families and, since we had no income apart from our salaries, none of us ever became rich and were thus relieved of the temptation to indulge in any form of ostentation. We were not status seekers in the social sense and 'status symbols' would have been meaningless to us even if the term had been invented at the time."

You could say that in all of this Andrews was being self-serving, that we should not trust peoples' accounts of their own motives. Yet consider for a moment what happened in 1970 when Todd Andrews was chairman of the RTE Authority and his son David was appointed as Fianna Fáil Chief Whip. In an equivalent situation these days, you can see the lines that would be trotted out: the chief whip doesn't make policy for Fianna Fáil and the chaiman of RTE doesn't make programmes, and anyway, if a matter of sensitivity ever arose, the chairman could always leave the room while it was being discussed. It didn't even occur to Todd Andrews to use any of these lines. He immediately resigned as chairman of RTE "rather than risk a situation that might give rise to a conflict of interest." No casuistry, no double-speak, no assumption that the limit of one's responsibility as a public person is the limitation of damage to one's own private position. Just the straightfoward reflex of humility that is triggered by the basic belief that there are public entities, things that are owned by all of us and are therefore greater than any of us.

If the people who set out to form the character of this state suffered from tunnel vision and self-righteousness, it needs to be observed that tunnel vision is still a kind ofvision and self-righteousness is still a kind of righteousness. Vision and righteousness — the idea of a future for a society and the idea that there is a morality at work in that society — are now confined to the dustbin of history, while the forward march of the nation is driven by one force and one force only — greed. Yet we need to recall what DeValera said, that "the essential thing in any state is not the governmental framework but the standard of citizenship on which it rests." And what Ken Whitaker said in launching this state on the path of modern economic development: that the advantage which Ireland had in seeking economic growth lay not in material resources but in the patriotism, dedication, co-operativeness and skill of its people. Now that the standard of citizenship is sinking from sight and the qualities of patriotism, co-operative-ness and dedication can be dismissed as so much old-fashioned socialism, we need to reflect on where the whole project of this state has found itself.

If what Whitaker said is true — that there is a strong connection between economic growth and the capacity of the people to dedicate themselves to something bigger than private greed — then there is also a connection between the moral bankruptcy that is evident all around us and the economic bankruptcy that is even more evident. And if the instincts of people like De Valera and Andrews were right — that Fianna Fáil rests on some meaning being given to the the word "citizenship" — then there is also a connection between that moral crisis and the slow political crisis of present day Fianna Fáil. The point about the things we are seeing just now is not just that there may have been a betrayal of trust by some of those who exercise power in this state, but that there may have been a betrayal of themselves, of their own traditions, ideas and values.

It is not right to say that what we are seeing these days is the collapse of an old ethic and the rise of a new amorality. For we have also seen throughout the 1980's the rise of a new ethic, one that justifies itself in terms yet more mystical and irrationally religious than any old morality. In this new morality, whereby, as Ivan Boesky put it, you can be greedy and still feel guilty about yourself, Adam Smith's invisible Hand guides the selfish pursuit of self-interest on the part of the mighty towards the ultimate good of society. By some magic, the pursuit of private greed will pull the rest of us along with it, creating wealth, creating jobs, creating a better society for all. This ethic is now the official one, held to with a dogmatism unaffected by its patent failure to create the jobs that this country needs with a terrifying urgency. The Invisible Hand may well help those who pursue their self-interest with such determination to feel good about themselves but the shape of that hand is becoming increasingly clear: two fingers raised to the society as a whole, the rest crossed behind the back in the hope of not being found out. It is, luckily, a posture that is difficult to maintain for very long.

The untenability of that posture will be the hidden agenda behind today's meeting of the Fianna Fáil parliamentary party. Behind all the arguments and all their ramifications for the leadership will lie the question of how Fianna Fáil, almost without knowing it, stopped being a civil rights movement and became the K Klub Klan. The Republican Party has to ask itself whether, in ditching much of its capital R Republicanism, it didn't also ditch the other, the older and grander, notion of the republic as a community of political equals in which the aristocracy of wealth has no more place than the old aristocracy of title and inheritance. What disturbs most people is not a sense of outrage at any individual act of corruption or incompetence. No such acts have yet been shown clearly and unequivocally to have taken place. What disturbs people is the broader and less focussed sense that power and sovereignty in this country do not derive from the people, as they are meant to do in a democratic republic, but from an anarchic greed that has gone out of control. In that sense the present crisis is not just an ethical or even an economic one, it is also a profoundly political one, exposing as it does a basic malfunction in the entire political mechanism of the state. After 70 years this state finds itself right back at the start, asking the same questions which lead to its foundation in the first place: where does political power properly come from and how is it properly used?

3.

November, 1991. Haughey survives a challenge to his leadership by Albert Reynolds, but is clear that his departure is now inevitable.

Perhaps the most significant statement in all the millions of words that have been spoken about the future of Charles Haughey in recent days was that of the Fianna Fáil TD, Michael Martin. Talking about the challenge to the leadership on radio, Michael Martin said that if Mr. Haughey were to be dumped without ceremony and dignity, the result would be that Fianna Fáil would become just another political party and cease to be a great national movement. It is on the face of it an extraordinary statement and an extaordinary fear: that a political party might come to be regarded as a political party. It is hard to think of a governing party anywhere outside of the Third World (and even there the ideology of the "national movement" is falling apart) which would be so terrified of appearing to be what it so obviously is. And yet, in saying this, Michael Martin was putting his finger on precisely what is at issue for his party as it meets today. To understand this strange distinction between political party and national movement is to understand the place of Charles Haughey, the brilliance of his achievement for his party and the immense difficulty which Fianna Fáil faces in finding a safe path to a future without him.

It is hard for outsiders not steeped in the culture of Fianna Fáil to understand the crucial distinction between a national movement and a political party as it is for Muslims to grasp the distinction between transubstantiation and consubstantiation in Christian theology. And indeed the theological analogy is a good one, because we're dealing here with something essentially religious in impulse. In its own ideology, Fianna Fáil is the temporal wing of a spiritual entity. The first line of its constitution says that "Fianna Fáil is a National Movement" (note the capital letters) and only subsequently goes on to state that "The movement shall be organised and known as Fianna Fáil The Republican Party." Just as the catechism taught us that a sacrament is the outward sign of a state of grace, so Fianna Fáil as a party is the outward sign of an inner state of political grace.

You can understand how this kind of mystical notion of politics could have arisen out of the torments and yearnings of the years surrounding the foundation of the state, but it is much more difficult to understand how it could still survive in the mouth of a young, intelligent TD in 1990s Ireland. To see it's survival, to understand the strength that the survival has given to Fianna Fáil and to say that Charles Haughey has been the crucial factor in it, is to begin to assess his meaning for his party with some fairness. For the truth is that it is not fair to see Mr. Haughey as a man who took over a party at the height of its powers and turned it into a failing and faction-ridden power machine. It is closer to the truth to say that he took over a party whose fundamental ideology and governing rhetoric was in deep trouble and somehow managed to sustain it in power. You can look at the Haughey leadership two ways: you can say that he took something strong and made it weak, or you can say that he took something virtually unsustainable and kept it going. His ability to maintain the myth of the National Movement suggests that the latter perspective comes closer to getting it right than the former.

Fianna Fáil's mysticism has always been peculiarly practical, and the National Movement ideology has had huge practical benefits for the party. If you are not a mere political party then you don't have to explain yourself in the same way. You don't have to give the game away about whose interests you want to represent. By attaching yourself to a beautiful abstraction like the Nation, you can be on everybody's side, the rich and the poor, the farmer and the urban worker, and whatever you're having yourself. In his now famous 1981 Ard-Fheis address, Mr. Haughey told the faithful in strikingly religious terms, that they got the support of the people because Fianna Fáil "represents not this pressure group or that sectional interest, this class or that creed, but because in the broad sweep of its membership and their faith and devotion to their own country, there resides what one can well call 'the spirit of the nation'."

The Spirit of the Nation does not need to argue or explain. The party does not justify itself to the people, is not accountable, because it is the people, or at least the people who matter, the real Irish people. "This Ard-Fheis," Mr. Haughey told his congregation in 1984, " speaks with the authentic voice of Irish Ireland." And for a long time, this authentic voice of Irish Ireland could be merged with P.J. Mara's Una Voce, Uno Duce. As Ray Burke, this time the first cock to crow, declared in 1982 during one of the heaves: "Loyalty to Fianna Fáil is loyalty to the nation itself and it's social and economic progress." And since loyalty to the party was loyalty to it's leader, then disloyalty to the person of Charles Haughey was an act of treason against the nation.

To outside commentators, the divisive nature of the Haughey persona was taken as a sign of the damage he was doing to Fianna Fáil. In fact, that divisiveness was the very thing that kept the National Movement notion alive. Fianna Fáil has always depended on a mental division of the populace into real people and others. Haughey gave this division new life by creating pro-Charlie and anti-Charlie camps. The passions aroused by Mr. Haughey recreated and reaffirmed a Fianna Fáil world view which would otherwise have been impossible to sustain in the face of increasingly corporate and managerial styles of government.

Nor were the uses of the National Movement confined to Fianna Fáil's internal sense of itself. It was crucial in maintaining the extraordinary alliance of classes on which Fianna Fáil survives. As a National Movement, Fianna Fáil could at once disavow ideology and, when necessary, claim to be the real socialist party. It was "the party of practical socialism" (Brian Lenihan), made up of "pragmatists of the centre" (Charles Haughey), "the workers' political party" (Patrick Hillery), even, in a superbly ambivalent phrase, "a radical, left of centre, free enterprise party" (Erskine Childers). Ironically, for a party which has seen itself as the opposite of all things English, this deft ideology was like nothing so much as a native version of Disraeli's One Nation Toryism.

As Mrs. Thatcher demonstrated with a vengeance, One Nation Toryism is all very well when there is enough in the kitty to keep everyone mildly happy, but when times get tough it is quickly abandonned in favour of the class war. Fianna Fáil the Workers' Party came to a sticky end amidst health cuts, the unemployment crisis and the rise of the spirit of the K Club. As we emerge as a classic one third/two thirds society, the pretence that we are One Nation can no longer be maintained. Only the power of the Haughey personality to provoke fervent loyalty on the one hand and fierce hatred on the other could disguise the fact that the real divisions were far from those of pro-Charlie and anti-Charlie camps, of National Movement and shoneens. The free enterprise socialist is a sleight-of-hand and Charles Haughey was Fianna Fáil's Marvo. Now that he has no more rabbits to pull from the hat, who else is there who can manage the trick?

It is not just a question of whether Fianna Fáil will try to sustain the Fianna Fáil the Workers' Party image with Bertie Ahern (Brian Lenihan might have managed it had things not fallen apart for him), or will go for the hard-nosed Eurocrat managerial style of Albert Reynolds or Ray MacSharry. The problem with all of the above and even more so with Mary O'Rourke is that they are leaders of political parties, not of the National Movement. There has been so much criticism of Charlie Haughey's divisiveness that it has not been clear that the problem for any potential successor to his mantle is that none of them is divisive enough. If the National Movement depends on a quasi-religious view of the political world as divided into the elect and the damned, Fianna Fáil no longer posesses a figure capable of sustaining interest in that division. The idea of Irish politics as a permanent fixture between Fianna Fáil and a World XV has already been shattered by the coalition with the P.Ds. After Haughey, the language of the National Movement will have to go too. It is not so long ago, after all, that Des O'Malley was saying things like "Ireland is one island, one nation, because God made it so." Now the rest of his former colleagues will have to live without the comfort of that rhetoric as he has learned to do. Far from the PDs rejoining Fianna Fáil, Fianna Fáil will have to rejoin the PDs.

4.

February 1992. With the Progressive Democrats threatening to resign from Government over allegations from the former Minister for Justice Sean Doherty that Charles Haughey knew of his tapping of the phones of journalists in the early 1980s, Haughey finally announces his intention to resign at a Fianna Fáil parliamentary party meeting.

Nothing is more pompous, and few thing are more untrue, than the cliché that "the Irish people will not lightly forgive anyone who causes an unnecessary general election at this point in time." It may well be that the precise opposite is true, that, deep down, we find it hard to forgive those who deny us the one remaining and undisputed power of Irish Politics: its ability to give us lots of elections.

One of the reasons the Progressive Democrats, for instance, are widely admired but not widely liked is their terrible habit of dangling the prospect of elections in front of us and then snatching the promised treat away. Conversely, the reason Charles Haughey is widely liked but not widely admired is that there is one ground on which he has never failed us: entertainment.

The images that will survive in the mind from the last week are images of entertainment not of political ideas;

the old footage of Albert Reynolds in cowboy suit singing. *Put Your Sweet Lips A Little Closer To The Phone*, the deep concern among the populace about what would become of Dermot Morgan and *Scrap Saturday* if they did not have Charlie to kick around any more.

The images on the television news of reporters and photographers hanging around the Dail gates while the meeting was in progress listening to ... *Scrap Saturday*. and Gerry Collin's splendidly funny performance on the *Six-One News*.

In more ways than one we have been making a show of ourselves, and whatever you think about the finale, the show itself is terrific. "Yes, We Have No Successors" is an old favourite by now , but it will take a lot to make us tire of it.

If you compare the scenes outside the Dail on Saturday with the equivalent scenes from the heaves of the early 1980s, you can see just how much we have relaxed with the idea of politics as entertainment.

Then, the tension was real, the dangers were apparent, the feeling that the mob at the gates was a real part of a real process, the visible sign of the forces that lay behind Mr. Haughey, was inescapable. You felt that if things went badly (which is to say against Mr. Haughey) then violence of some sort was not an unthinkable possibility. Something was being fought out on those streets as well as inside the committee rooms.

This time, it could not have been more different. There were partisans in the crowd, but they were outnumbered by onlookers, revellers, participants in the carnival. If there was a potential for violence, it was the potential for the violence of a drunken New Year crowd at the cathedral, not of a political demonstration.

For most of the people there, the whole thing was clearly and consciously a show. And the star of the show was not Mr. Reynolds or Mr. Haughey, but the representative of the media on earth, Charlie Bird. This Charlie was serenaded and slagged, egged on.

The cries of "Charlie Bird for Taoiseach" were a part of the burlesque nature of the whole occasion, but they were not entirely without point. If the medium is the message, then the messenger is at the centre of events.

That style is now the real substance of our politics was emphasised by whatever debate there was around the leadership of Mr. Haughey. There was no serious discussion about unemployment or economic growth or the health services or the North. There were not even any detailed allegations against Mr. Haughey himself and his personal conduct.

Instead, there was unease about the style of leadership, the way in which certain radio interviews went, the public perception of things.

There was a rare moment of television in the days when Vaclav Havel was in spite of himself, begining to move from playwright to politician. He let the cameras of BBC's *The Late Show* follow him around. At one point, after a hectic day of meetings, public addresses, the whole business of projecting himself and saying very serious things about his country, the camera followed him into a bedroom where he sat on the bed and laughed, and laughed, at the infinitely comic notion of himself doing all these things.

It would be comforting to think that Gerry Collins had a good laugh at the sight of himself on television last week, or that Padraig Flynn had to go out to the toilet for a good hoot after listening to the sound of his own voice in the party room referring to himself in the third person.

Comforting, but not really of much help. For what matters is not the inner eye of the politician but the outer countenance, the style and apparent sincerity with which the game is played.

Rather than personality politics, what is at stake is the politics of personality. What we have to come to terms with is that there is almost nothing personal about political personalities. The idea of the political personality which we still work with is the classic 19th century liberal one which derives from the separation of the public and private spheres, the state on the one hand, society on the other.

In this notion, politics is what happens when responsible individuals meet in the public domain to give form and to shape public opinion. In this notion, politics is shaped above all by personal contact, the process of debate and argument which go towards making public opinion.

This notion, unfortunately doesn't work anymore. There is no longer a division between the public sphere and the private sphere, at least not an absolute one. For one thing, the state has taken over many of the functions of the family, and is thus as much a part of private life as it is of public life.

For another thing, the mass media, and in particular television, manage to create a kind of public life that does not have to involve personal contact at all. We receive most of our images of public life not in public, but in private, in our own sitting rooms.

What this means is that we consume these images rather than help create them. And, as we know from watching television, a synthetic image may be actually better for consumption than a real one. A man getting shot in a movie may often be better, more carefully constructed, image than a news recording of the same thing.

And just as television ads have invented the idea of fictional authority (the man in the white coat telling you that his brand of dental floss is more effective than any other is not a real scientist, and we know he isn't, but he still has an air of authority), so it is with politics. Being authoritative is about how you look, how you dress, how you use the techniques of television, and not about the truth or otherwise of what you are saying.

The issue, as it arose for Fianna Fáil, is not whether Mr. Haughey was lying about this, that or the other, but about whether he appeared to be lying, whether he has lost his, in this sense fictional, authority.

As an electorate, we have become very sophisticated about all this. We know that the link between what our political leaders do and what they say is a matter of form rather than of reality. And since that is the game we have ceased to expect such a link.

We don't fundamentally believe that they will create jobs/end poverty/stop the violence/reform taxation, or whatever. But we do enjoy the endless and increasingly daring game of *Call My Bluff* in which they have to convince us that they are being "credible" about all these things.

As the gap widens, the game gets more and more thrilling. It is entertainment of a very high order, and we love it. It is, this ability to entertain us, the one thing on which they have never let us down.

5.

February 1992. Albert Reynolds is about to be elected Taoiseach.

Long before he got to be Taoiseach, Albert Reynolds ruled more lands than Genghis Khan: Cloudland, Roseland, Fairyland, Barrowland, Rockland, Borderland, Moyland. Those are, of course, the names of the ballrooms from which he made his fortune. While it may be that he is not the first Irish political leader to have ruled, even to have inhabited, Dreamland and Cloudland, there is something particular about a Fianna Fáil leader who could make so light of the party's raison d'être, partition, as to believe that Borderland was just a dancehall in Clones.

Assuming that he keeps his appointment date with history, Albert Reynolds will be the first leader of that party to have a background not in the clash of the ash or the echo of the Thompson gun, but in the flash of the cash and some mean ticky-tacky drumming from the Melody Aces. While Charles Haughey's achievement was to bridge the gap between the rhetoric of Fianna Fáil's national aspirations and the realities of an enthusiastically materialist culture, there is, for Albert, no such gap. He has always been on the far side of that divide, an inhabitant, and indeed a creator of the new pragmatic Republic.

Albert Reynolds's origins in the showband boom are a source of great mirth to those of us who grew up on Woodstock and glam rock rather than Woodbines and Dicky Rock. But they shouldn't be. Albert Reynolds was more of a social revolutionary when he was running dancehalls than he has been as a political leader.

I am not being facetious when I say that Albert Reynolds's most important contribution to modern Ireland, aside from the modernisation of the phone system, is the introduction of the first £1000 bingo session. The historic night was December 15th, 1963. The place was the Roseland Ballroom in Moate. It was naturally enough packed, and Albert made more than £1000 profit on the night.The night deserves its place in the history books, because it is as important in a way as the *First Programme For Economic Expansion*. If you're tacitly abandoning the great national aspirations to a frugal, unified, monolithic, non-materialistic society, then what dream do you put in its place? The dream of course, that everyone can make a fortune, that we can all strike it lucky. Two fat ladies and legs 11 took the place of Ireland not merely free but Gaelic as well. That became, in effect our political ideology, and our politicans have been shouting out numbers ever since.

Nor is a backround of booking showbands to be seen as somehow infra dig for a Fianna Fáil leader. It is not accidental that there has long been a connection that reached its apotheosis in Mr. Haughey's recent description of Reynolds, Flynn & Co as "the country and western alliance." The showband boom was the result of the application of Fianna Fáil's political methods to the business of entertainment.

Fianna Fáil was, above all, a map of the Republic, an abstracted model of the contours of the 26 Counties, made up of an immense amount of local knowledge and intimate detail about the specific characteristics of this or that place. The famous *Radharc* documentary of the 1960s, in which Neil Blaney and his assistants could stand on a hill and give a complete description of the political landscape below them, in terms of the voting allegiances of every household, is the classic image of this phenomenon. Albert Reynolds, it is well to remember, learned all his politics from working with Blaney in the by-elections of the 1960s. And his success with dancehalls came from exactly the same way of using local knowledge.

The Reynolds chain of ballrooms was a country all to itself, stretching from New Ross to Clones and from Ballina to Athy. And you had to know that country as well as Fianna Fáil knew Ireland. You had to know that Tuesday was a good night in Mullingar, Wednesday in Portlaois, Thursday in Roscommon, Friday in Limerick and Athy. You had to know that the Melody Aces would have them packed as tight as TDs at a parish priest's funeral in Moate, but stick them into Athy where the punters thought they were too sophisticated to dance to such country clods, and you'd be left with enough space on the floor to please a team of fancy Russian ice-skaters. Compared to his later business of pet food, where you only had to figure out what nine out of ten cats prefer, this required of Albert Reynolds an immensely sophisticated knowledge of the state he would one day lead.

It is a belief in this knowledge that has led Fianna Fáil to the brink of entrusting its future into the hands of Albert Reynolds. The party knows that it lost its map of the Republic, that the day Charles Haughey went on the radio and said that he hadn't realised that people were so upset about health cuts was the day Fianna Fáil had to realise with a shock that it was now running a foreign country. In choosing Albert Reynolds to lead it, the party is placing its faith in his ability to know which is the right night in Mullingar and which in Rooskey, which band will go down well with the voters in Clones and which will pack them in Darndale. It is leaving behind the party of aspirations once and for all and going for the party of pragmatism. It is leaving behind the party of visions, and going for the party of keen eyes and quick calculations. It is giving up the articulation of national hopes and going instead for the skill of giving the people what they want.

In doing so, Fianna Fáil is making a very big mistake. The mistake is to believe that just because the tired rhetoric of the spirit of the nation doesn't work any more the Irish people don't want leaders who can articulate real and concrete aspirations. Fianna Fáil's apparent belief that by getting itself into organisational shape, losing its dodgy image and employing a skilled judge of what the people want it can solve its problems, is misplaced. Fianna Fáil gave us the £1000 bingo that is a modern free enterprise economy, and we like it. But we also have learned that too many people lose and too many get left outside the hall. We remain full of the unarticulated gaps between what we are, what Fianna Fáil made us, and what we would like to be.

Those gaps can't be filled by someone taking us as we are and trying to devise strategies to keep us happy. We don't really know what we aspire to until someone invents a vision of it and puts it before us. What nine out of ten cats really prefer, as Albert Reynolds must know, is not to be bothered with market research, but to have their owners make interesting choices and present them for their acceptance or rejection. Mary Robinson did that, and Mary O'Rourke might have done. But I can't see Albert Reynolds doing so. When Mary Robinson said "Come dance with me in Ireland" and the people accepted the invitation, knowing what would fill a ballroom on a wet Tuesday night in Roosky was no part of the equation.

6.

November 1992. The general election campaign is going badly for Fianna Fáil.

Most things are marked by the circumstances of their creation and this election so far has been no exception. Because its initial subject has been the unsuitability of Fianna Fáil to coalition and its search for an overall majority, that has been the shape of the choice offered to us as voters.

Some choice. We are apparently being asked to pick either a majority Fianna Fáil administration, a prospect that has become quite chilling, or an absurd dolly mixture coalition of Fine Gael, Labour and the Progressive Democrats. It is the choice Henry Ford offered purchasers of the Model T — any colour you want so long as it's black. The possibilities opened up by this unacceptable choice are very black indeed.

We are in effect being asked to choose between slightly refurbished versions of the alternatives that have brought us to the terrible state we are in. On the one hand there is the Albert Factor, a less interesting remake of the Charlie Factor, but with all the same questions about credibility. On the other, there is the right-left coalition which, from experience, tends to offer the worst of both worlds. It is a very poor choice for a country that has lurched into permanent crisis, a country whose society is hovering on a point of no return, to be offered.

In political terms, what is now happening is that both Fianna Fáil and Fine Gael are trying to pretend that what is now a five or six party system is still the old two and a half party system. The process of fragmentation that has gone on in Irish politics in the last decade is being ignored in the mutual desire to present the electoral choice as essentially one between an Albert Reynolds Government and a John Bruton Government. The sleight of hand suits both Fianna Fáil and Fine Gael, and their tacit understanding not to let the cat out of the bag on this one unites them in this election to a far greater degree than any substantial difference of policy divides them.

At a more profound level, though, this numbers game can be seen as a mere reflection of something deeper. It hides the fact that both of the major parties are in real long-term trouble. For most of the State's history, the Fianna Fáil v. Fine Gael model worked well as a way of providing Governments, even if it achieved little else. The strength of the polarity tended to mean that a loss for one of the parties meant a gain for the other. And because the parties themselves were effectively coalitions, there was as much to be gained in terms of political change by shifts within the parties as by shifts between them.

This is no longer the case. We are now in a situation in which both parties are in serious decline simultaneously. Fianna Fáil can no longer offer a realistic prospect of single-party Government. Fine Gael can no longer offer even a reasonable prospect of double-party Government. And this decline is ideological as well as electoral. Fianna Fáil's ideological culture has been deeply damaged. Fine Gael has gone into ideological reverse.

One of Fianna Fáil's big problems has been its failure to understand the ideological achievements of Charles Haughey. Because of his ability to survive at all costs, because of his capacity to change deeply-held ideological beliefs from month to month, the party seemed to forget what he had done for it in terms of bringing its political culture through years of massive social change. Haughey achieved something enormous in accommodating Fianna Fáil's traditional ideological roots to contemporary Ireland. The strains, the contradictions, the reversals, were a sign of the massive nature of his task, not, as they were taken to be, of the unimportance of ideology.

Fianna Fáil's hard men were by turns amused and irritated by Haughey's habit of surrounding himself with brilliant intellectuals like Anthony Cronin and Martin Mansergh, of, for instance, turning up to open Knock Airport with Paul Durcan in tow. When he started quoting Malraux, they smirked at his Medici-complex. They forgot that the Medicis, too, were hard men, men who understood that deciding what paintings to hang on the palace walls was as important in the retention of power as knowing where to place the knife between the shoulder blades.

In replacing Haughey, the hard men forgot the extent to which his "pragmatism" was made possible by the cultural, and indeed mystical, soup in which it swam. They forgot that pragmatism without a rich ideological dressing soon comes to taste like ruthlessness in the mouths of the electorate. They thought that a culture of clichés — "the buck stops here," "my door is always open" (and presumably "my path is free to walk"), "I'm a straight-forward guy and I tell it like it is" — could replace the careful ideological construct which was the house that Charlie built. They thought that a few country 'n' western standards could do for them what Yeats and Malraux and Cronin had done for Haughey. They thought that the way you influence the climate of opinion is to send writs to newspapers and veiled threats to RTE.

They were wrong, of course. Pragmatism without ideological artifice does come across as ruthlessness. Albert Reynolds has been a brilliantly pragmatic politician. Which is to say he has been extremely good at getting things done without counting the cost. As a member of the original Gang Of Five, he helped get rid of Jack Lynch, without counting the cost of narrowing Fianna Fáil's appeal. As the man who toppled Charles Haughey, he won the leadership of Fianna Fáil without counting the cost of losing Haughey's ideological suppleness. As Bertie Ahern's rival for the leadership, he destroyed his opponent, without counting the cost of undermining Ahern's popularity and weakening one of the party's great assets. As the victor in that contest, he ruthlessly punished his last challenger, Mary O'Rourke, without counting the cost of her intelligence and acumen to his Government.

Once in office, his pragmatism led to formidable achievements attained at very high cost. He bullied Maastricht through at the cost of a real debate about our place in Europe, and with the help of a disingenuous promise of £6 billion that will not arrive. He ruthlessly outflanked both the Pro-Life Campaign and the Catholic Church (more than a celebrated liberal like Garret FitzGerald ever managed), but at the cost of a horrendous constitutional amendement that will cause more grief and anguish in the future. And he survived the nightmare of having to give evidence to the beef tribunal, but at the cost of bringing down his own Government.

Such ruthless pragmatists are at their best in the politics of putsch and coup, and it is important to remember that Albert Reynolds has been central to three coups in his relatively short political career. One was against Jack Lynch, the second against Charles Haughey, and the latest and most bizarre was against his own coalition Government. All three were coups from the backwoods, made in the name of Fianna Fáil core values. All three had the effect of hardening up the Fianna Fáil culture, of galvanising the faithful.

Elections, however, are different to coups. Coups are carried out by hardening the line, but elections are won by softening it. The task in a modern election is not to capture your core vote, but to appeal to those who are not part of it. John Major won last year by softening Thatcherism. Bill Clinton won by softening Democratic liberalism. Albert Reynolds has done the opposite: he has galvanised Fianna Fáil, but also driven it back into its heartland. That heartland still beats, but it is simply no longer large enough to do what Mr Reynolds wants it to do — elect a majority Government.

Fine Gael, too, has been driven back into its core. The clusters which were gathered around that core by Garret FitzGerald — liberals, social democrats, feminists — have broken off as the party has moved to the right. The social democratic wing is in very deep trouble, as can be seen from the fact that the party's urban working class constituency has narrowed to a degree where it faces disaster in Dublin city if the local vote last year is a reliable guide. Its feminist constituency is also troubled, as evidenced by the poignant fact that its gain of Frances Fitzgerald last week was matched by its loss of a disillusioned Nuala Fennell.

Both major parties have become narrower. The result is that neither Fianna Fáil nor Fine Gael is in a position to create a genuine coalition of interests, as opposed to a cobbled-together coalition of parties. Their mutual rejection of the logical alternative — a coalition between them — is, in those circumstances, simply not good enough. The attractions of such a coalition — a logical divide in Irish politics between right and left, and a coalition arrangement in which there is no small party to be bullied — are far too great for the idea to be dismissed by both sides as something which wouldn't wash with their supporters. Both parties have to learn that what matters now is not what will wash with their own supporters, but what will wash with an electorate that has a continually decreasing desire to be numbered in that category.

7.

December 1992. Fianna Fáil has had its worst election result for decades.

Eamon de Valera famously said that "whenever I wanted to know what the Irish people wanted, I had only to examine my own heart and it told me straight off what the Irish people wanted." Last week, the Irish people performed a by-pass operation on de Valera's heart.

When he spoke these words, they were not as absurd as they now seem. He was defending himself against the charge that as a "foreigner" he was not fit to represent the people of Clare and the Irish people. In seeking to vindicate himself he appealed to his childhood, to its Irishness, its purity, its deep roots in what we are. His vision of an Irish childhood was so convincing that he led us for four decades after that speech.

Last week, the people of Dev's old constituency elected a South African born socialist of Indian descent. They clearly did not regard him as a foreigner merely because his childhood had not been spent here. It was his adulthood, not his childhood, that mattered. They said for the first time that what made you Irish was hard adult experience, not a dim and golden childhood of fond memories. And in that shift from a Clare candidate elected for his childhood to one elected for his adulthood lies an appropriate enough metaphor for what we have been through in the past week.

Perhaps the most significant thing about the election is not the result, but the mood that the result represents. That mood is a mood of change, but a strikingly sober one as well. If there is a new dawn, it is also winter, and in the Irish winter dawns are generally grey and drizzly, a modulation in the shades of darkness rather than a burst of new colour. Everybody knows too clearly that it is despair, not wild hope, that has forced this change. Everybody knows that if the Irish political system is at last growing up, the price of growing up is a loss of illusion.

Fianna Fáil lost its illusions first. The most astonishing thing about the election was that Fianna Fáil's campaign was determined in significant ways by a 23-year old English Tory. Stephen Hilton was brought to Áras de Valera from Conservative Central Office via Saatchi and Saatchi. His strategy — copycat ads attacking Labour as the "tax and spend" party, stolen directly from the Tory campaign that was successful in the British election last

199

April — dominated the entire last week of Fianna Fáil's campaign.

Just think about that for a moment: Fianna Fáil, the party that used to look into its own heart to know what we were thinking, spent the last week before the Irish people went to the polls speaking in the voice of a young Tory spin-doctor who is practically straight out of Oxford. And they now wonder why they lost 10 seats.

The disillusion that lies behind that desperate tactic for Fianna Fáil only becomes fully clear when you think further about the Saatchi tactic that Fianna Fáil genuinely believed was the best hope it had of communicating its message to us. The thinking was explained in *The Guardian* by John Maples, the former Tory Treasury Minister who now works with Hilton in Saatchi's "election management" team (their clients include, as well as Fianna Fáil, the South African National Party, and the Turkish government). Maples said that his team was quite happy to work in any country "where the game is played pretty much as it is here," ie in Britain. "We felt," he said, "we had developed some techniques which were not country-specific but can be applied in any election campaign."

Not country-specific. Fianna Fáil spent the last week of a campaign in the grip of political advertising techniques that are not country-specific. The great national movement, the Spirit of the Nation, the party of Irish Ireland, the Soldiers of Destiny? Not country-specific. The boys with the calculators who could probably tell you now which Fianna Fáil families in which streets in Mullingar voted for Labour this time? Not country-specific. The lads who had spent their lives going to every donkey derby and dinner dance to keep an eye on everything that moved? Not country-specific.

This is the real political earthquake. Fianna Fáil actually thought that it was living in a country "where the game is played pretty much as it is" in Finchley and

Edgebaston and Dagenham. Otherwise, it would not have spent its money, and, more importantly, its precious time in the last days of an election, aping the Tories. In other words, it had definitively lost its faith and its illusions. That Ireland We Dreamed Of might just as well have been That Turkey We Dreamed Of, with comely dervishes dancing at the casbah. This is disillusionment on an epic scale.

If it had stopped to think for a moment, the party would have understood that if it was so disillusioned, then so, probably, was most of the electorate. And negative advertising is unlikely to work on people who have few illusions. Nobody really thinks that Labour is going to solve everybody's problems and give us peace, justice and plenty for Christmas. What swung the electorate to the left was not illusions, but a sober and healthy disillusionment.

What we are disillusioned with is the succession of formulae that are too petty for our problems. The illusion that cutting PRSI for employers, or performing a magic trick with borrowing that isn't borrowing, or waiting for the economic "climate" to change, is sufficient for the country in the state that we're in, doesn't wash anymore. Most of all the illusion that the right course is always down the middle of the road is gone.

What we saw last Wednesday was the disappearing middle. We saw a middle class that didn't feel in the middle anymore. The urban middle class no longer feels comfortably sandwiched between riches and deprivation, no longer expects to be tucked up warm and safe between unemployment and affluence. The thought that you might lose your job or your house, that your children might tumble into the abyss of unemployment however good a job you've done on their future, has broken the spell of permanent comfort.

Having tended to see the State as the people who take your hard-earned money and give it to the poor, the middle class has woken up to the fact that it itself is the main beneficiary from State spending. Labour has become the party of the State, both in terms of capturing the mantle of Good Government from Fine Gael, and in terms of protecting social welfare, social expenditure and public sector employment. The middle class has understood that it cannot protect itself without also protecting the mechanisms that are in place to protect the unemployed and the poor.

Similarly, in the abortion referendums, we saw the failure of the formula that has always worked for Fianna Fáil: splitting the difference. Fianna Fáil has always pursued the Golden Mean, the belief that the shortest distance between any two points was precisely half way between them. The "right to life" clause was based on the belief that something half-way between the "extremes" of anti-abortion and pro-choice campaigns was bound to be right simply because it was in the middle. It failed. That middle, too, has disappeared.

The lesson of this disappearing middle is that the parties, when they finally begin talks on the formation of a government, must not be content to try to reproduce it. Splitting the difference between privatisation and state enterprise, between active job creation and climatology, between justice and laissez faire, will simply not work. There is no stable middle ground to appeal to anymore, no comfortable centre to be Saatchurated into accepting the status quo, and anyone who wants to try might as well hire Stephen Hilton now.

THE IRELAND WE HOPE
TO LEAVE BEHIND

"There were seven of us in the family, two boys and five girls. I was the eldest. My father was a founder-member of the Gardai. He took part in the war of Independence, the Civil War, and then was in the Gardai from the start. He was the only son of a farmer from Swanlinbar in Co. Cavan, and while he was on the run, his mother died. An RIC man and two Black and Tans came looking for him, beat up my grandfather, burnt the place, shot the dog that used to go out after the cattle. So he didn't go back to the land. He joined the guards straight away and stayed in it all his life. You could say it was his life.

"He took the Free State side and was part of the contingent that took over Athlone with General Sean MacEoin. Then he was sent to Boyle, where he met my mother. Even when things were vicious in the civil War, he wasn't. A well-known Free State character, Dockery, was shot in Boyle, so close up that there were burns on his face. The Free State army fellas were furious at this and they had some prisoners there and they decided to execute one of them. My father, who was a young powerful man — he was six feet two — disarmed his fellow Free State people at great risk to himself and saved this fellow. Subsequently, when he was a guard in Ballinmore, still during the civil war, he was cycling down a lane way one day when he was ambushed by three fellas and they were going to execute him. And it transpired that when they found out his name, one of the three fellas was a brother of the chap that my father had saved. It was one of those strange coincidences. And as a result, they let my father go. There was some kind of simple justice at work after all.

"After all this, when things settled, he was stationed in a town in east Mayo, and things were grand for a long

203

time.One night in 1937, he was on night duty and was passing this pub. There were lights on so he went in and raided it. Unfortunately, it was after a Fianna Fáil cumann meeting. He got a decent respectable businessman, a draper who was our next-door neighbour, as well as a crowd of latchicos. And this was the problem. It was alright for the businessman to associate with these fellas at a cumann meeting, but for it to come out in a public court that he had been drinking with them after hours was not permissable.

"My father was told to drop the case, but he wouldn't. He was a very simple man. He was a conservative Irish Catholic and he thought he was doing what he had sworn to do when he took up his job. So he was immediately transferred to Achill Island, where there was a great disturbance going on at the time over the free milk scheme and a guard had been badly beaten up. In other words, a danger area. From there, we were transferred to Glenamoy, so remote a place that there wasn't even a national school for miles. And we were of an age where we needed secondary schools.

"There was no way he could afford to keep us with him and send us to boarding schools. He was on about £3 10s a week. So we kids had to go to Ballina with my mother where we could get to schools.

"The day we were transferred first will always be in my mind. I will never, ever forget us standing in that street, loading up my father's chattels on the back of a little lorry. When the time came to say goodbye, my little sister was missing. We went to look for her and we eventually found her in the house of a man who was having my father transferred, a Fianna Fáil councillor, afterwards chairman of the county council, playing with his daughter.

"That sister of mine subsequently died. She was a fine big healthy girl, very bright at school, and it was one of those things that would only need a few days in hospital. During the period she was ill, like all the rest of the time, my father was allowed home for 24 hours every month. He would have to cycle the 32 miles in and back, between Glenamoy and Ballina, on sandy, potholed roads. It took four hours each way, which meant he had 16 hours with us a month. He could be with her only a minimal period of time. When she did die, he stayed for the funeral and got a taxi-car back to work which he couldn't afford at all. But he was three hours late reporting back for duty and the superintendent had come all the way out from Belmullet to check him in. He was reprimanded and fined.

"It hit us financially, because the rent allowance for the town was £48 a year, and for Glenamoy was only £12 a year and we had to pay both for the family in Ballina and into the mess in Glenamoy. But that was only a small part of it. The emotional effect was shocking. You hadn't a father, all of a sudden. And it has never left me. I was 13 years old when we were transferred, and I was watching the whole thing; us being hunted out of a town with our goods and chattels out on the street, on the back of the lorry, like tinkers, our whole life changed so much. I was at the stage where I needed my father, and so did my sisters, a firm guiding hand. The effect on me was devastating, that I hadn't anybody there. It's a lifelong thing: you always feel what you missed. The whole family was broken by it really.

"The man was humiliated to the extreme degree for doing what he had pledged to do. It must have been difficult for him to comprehend. He was a conservative man who said the rosary every night, strict religious duty, did the first Fridays, right to the end. He seemed to accept it better than I did, at least he kept up the pretence. He never talked about it much. But what haunts me is that I don't know whether he accepted it or not, because I never knew my father. He died and we never knew him. He was a figure who appeared once a month, and even then he was trying to set the vegetables in the garden or cut turf, towards helping the family. There was no time for fun or affection.

"When people started to joke about it, when they had Brian Lenihan on the *Late Late Show* and they were telling stories about a guard being asked if he wanted a drink or a transfer when they were caught drinking after hours, it really opened a sore for me. It was supposed to be funny, but it's horrible, horrible to me and a lot of other Gardai families as well. What's so funny about having your father made a stranger and your family devastated? Maybe people should think about that, and see what effect it has on their sense of humour."

I was told that story a few days ago, a few days before we inaugurate a new president. The man was quiet and calm and dignified. He is 66 years of age, and he doesn't shout or rant or curse, but in the set of his eyes and the clench of his hands as he tells that story there is living pain that will not die until he does. I wrote the story down because I hope, in the next few days, it willl have become history, and history should be written down lest we forget it. How can we know that we are changing for the better if not by marking where we are coming from and feeling free to say in truth: "At least we know that sort of thing will not happen again?"

Irish Times, November 1990

LARRY

Of all the things said by Larry Goodman in the course of three days of evidence to the beef tribunal last week, one small, offhand remark may be the most significant. Significant, that is, not for the finding of facts which is Mr Justice Hamilton's job, but for the broader illumination of Irish society which is the inevitable by-product of such sustained concentration on one small aspect of it. Sometimes it is the parentheses, the crumbs of speech that drop from the table, that say more than all the carefully phrased expositions and explanations.

The phrase that caught the ear came early in Mr Goodman's evidence, when he was explaining that, yes, whenever he wanted something done he would go straight to the top, to the Minister or the Taoiseach. His habit of doing so, he said, was something that "didn't endear me to the establishment."

A world view opened itself up in those words, allowing us a brief and rare glimpse into the way power in Ireland tends to see itself. Here was a man who had controlled nearly five per cent of the country's Gross National Product. One pound in every 20 generated in the country had passed through his hands. And if you leave out the multinationals, whose economic power in Ireland is not essentially an Irish exercise of power, Mr Goodman's weight in the country was far greater than even this figure would suggest. He was selling 1.3 million head of cattle a year, more than the annual total slaughtered in Ireland. His main business had a turnover approaching the billion pound mark. And all of this was done through a private company, unanswerable even to public shareholders.

Yet he was not, in his own eyes, a part of "the establishment." He may have controlled Ireland's most important export industry. He may have been able to leave instructions for the Minister for Industry and Commerce to ring him at home over the weekend and be confident that they would be carried out. He may have had regular and personal access to the machinery of government from the Taoiseach down. He may have had an Irish embassy and the Department of Foreign Affairs writing notes on the importance of not making him angry. But none of this made him a part of the establishment.

In Ireland, for people with power, the establishment is always someone else. It is nebulous, invisible, a faceless but malevolent force that is always out to stop "us" from doing all the wonderful things we would surely do if only we were left to our own devices. Everybody with power sees encircling enemies everywhere. Bishops believe that there is a secular media establishment working away to undermine them. Anti-abortionists, many of them in control of powerful institutions, see themselves as threatened by a dark conspiracy of the establishment to foist abortion on the Irish people. Politicians in office, including some who have held power for years, see themselves as victims of sinister conspiracies. And Mr Goodman, one of the richest and most powerful men in the country, sees himself as an outsider victimised by an establishment to which he failed to endear himself.

In some ways, the situation in Ireland is not unlike that amongst the nomenclature of the old Communist bloc. Because those with power had acquired it out of the dispossession of an old establishment, they were able to see power and privilege as something that, by defintion, belonged to the old enemy, and to remain blind to their own position as the new establishment. In Ireland, the revolutionary movement slowly worked its way into the nooks and crannies of power and privilege, but retained the sense of itself as being the representative of the victimised and oppressed, and therefore as being itself still victimised by "the establishment."

Because there is, in Ireland, a self-conscious élite created by a certain number of fee-paying schools, to be outside of that élite, however much power and wealth and control of other peoples' lives you may have, is to be allowed the luxury of feeling yourself to be outside of the establishment. A neat kind of negative logic operates.

The establishment talks through its noses. I talk through the side of my mouth, therefore I am not a member of the establishment. The establishment has yachts. I have a helicopter, therefore I am not part of the establishment. The establishment went to Clongowes and graduated from university debating societies. I went to the Christian Brothers and left school at 14 to start my own business, therefore I am not an establishment type. The establishment lives in redbrick houses in Dublin 4. I live in El Ponderoso on 900 acres, therefore I am not one of them. The establishment likes opera. I have my chauffeur put Foster and Allen on the stereo in the Merc, therefore I am a man of the people.

Ireland doesn't have much of what the English call "society" (an oxymoron if ever there was one), but it does have just enough to allow the truly powerful to feel good about not being part of it. We have a parody of "society" created rather than reflected by the social columns in the newspapers, the best of which, Terry Keane's in the *Sunday Independent*, is a delightful parody of a social column in which send-up and flattery are indistinguishable. Not being in the social columns is a much more comforting state for the truly powerful than being in them, allowing you to remain a perpetual outsider, even though the circle from which you are excluded is merely drawn in lipstick on a disposable tissue.

All the while, power proceeds, not through "society," but on its own quiet, simple way, not illuminated by flashbulbs, but in unrecorded, private meetings. And the joy of not being part of the establishment is that you are not responsible. If things go wrong, it is because the establishment is out to get you. If things go right, it is in spite of the obstacles the establishment has put in your way.

You might think that after 70 years of independent statehood we would have lost the notion that the establishment in Ireland was made up of West Brits and Castle Catholics. You might think that we had got used to the idea that power is as likely to be wielded in Ireland by Christian Brothers boys and country and western fans as it is by Jesuit-educated chaps who hang out at the yacht club. In particular, you might think that we'd grown up beyond the ridiculous notion that the establishment is a sensitive creature that cannot live outside of its natural urban habitat and is so incapable of surviving in the provinces that it shrivels up long before it gets to Maynooth. But it seems that we haven't, that power and responsibility remain a function of the outward appearances of class and status, and not of the real control which individuals exercise over others' lives.

For a long time now, we have had a State. That State, like any other, is kept going by the interaction of political, economic, religious and media power centres. Within this structure, a small number of individuals has access to economic power to an entirely disproportionate degree. About a fifth of the household wealth in Ireland is owned by the top one per cent of the population.

We can argue as much as we like about whether or not this is a tolerable situation and, if not, what should be done about it. But no coherent political programme — left, right, or centre — is possible until the idea that this place took responsibility for itself a long time ago is accepted. So long as politicians who have been in power are allowed to talk as if they have no responsibility for the immediate past, so long as churchmen are allowed to decry the state of a public morality that has been in their own hands for generations, and so long as immensely powerful businessmen are allowed to think of themselves as victimised outsiders, so long will the chances of this place being taken by the scruff of the neck remain very slim.

MYTH THAT LETS DUBLIN 4 EVADE ITS RESPONSIBILITY

Things have come to a pretty pass when it becomes necessary to defend, or at least to enter a plea in mitigation for Dublin 4. The denizens of that mythical domain, whoever they may be, are nobody's idea of an oppressed minority. As invented by the late John Healy, Dublin 4 is shorthand for the snotty establishment of rich liberals which is the real power in the land.

Never mind that my Dublin 4 relations are sailors, dockers, clerical workers and housewives — almost the epitome of another stereotype, the salt-of-the-earth working class. Never mind the late John Kelly's insistence that his constituency workers came from Cork, Cavan, Monaghan and Mayo. Never mind that the savagers of Dublin 4 are themselves, typically, Dublin based media professionals. The image has taken hold and it has become a powerful vehicle for obfuscation, offering a wonderfully handy way of dressing up rusty reaction as anti-establishment elan.

The pity is that the cliché, as usual, hides something much more complex and interesting. By painting the Old South Dublin professional class as a simple ruling élite, the ham-fisted portrait misses its real character, what might be called the Discreet Anarchy of the Bourgeoisie.

You can sample this anarchic steak in the old élite for a fiver by buying John Kelly's book of speeches, *Belling the Cats*.

If you really want to understand what is mistakenly called Dublin 4, you have to start with the fact that it is a frustrated ruling élite. If you could go back a hundred years, you could find it as a new Catholic professional class, edging its nose ahead, accumulating, often with heroic effort, a modicum of education and cultivation, of power and privilege. But that modicum was vastly important for one obvious reason: Home Rule was coming.

"My grandmother," as Conor Cruise O'Brien recalled, "intended quite consciously, I believe, to preside over the birth of a new ruling class; those who would rule the country when Home Rule was won."

Not only in Dublin but all around the Republic (in James Dillon's Ballaghaderreen, for instance, or in John Redmond's Waterford) there was a new ruling-class-in-waiting. And then, out of a clear sky, a crowd of upstart Christian Brothers boys with Webley revolvers came and took it all away with the mad rising.

Thus was born that fascinating phenomenon — a well-established and in many ways, highly privileged upper middle class that, without being in any way economically discommoded, was politically usurped. History gave us that powerful and articulate élite that was yet in certain ways contemptuous of the state which it should have inherited but didn't.

If Robert Tressell's workers were Ragged-Trousered Philanthropists, these are Pinstripe Trousered Anarchists.

What we have is that strangest of phenomena, an anti-establishment establishment, well heeled and articulate certainly, but also with a deep seated sense of itself as a class of outsiders. It is not west British (indeed it has a fierce and old-fashioned nationalism — in John Kelly's vocabulary of political abuse, "aping the British" is the worst insult), but neither is it greatly comfortable with the Irish State as it came into being.

In John Kelly's speeches, for instance there is a wonderful disrespect, not just for Fianna Fáil, but for the very apparatus of state itself. It is one thing to mock at your political opponents, but this is something else entirely, something that might be expected from far-left subversives, but is not a little shocking coming from a professor of Jurisprudence, side kick of Liam Cosgrave in the law-and-order days and one time Attorney General.

You wouldn't be surprised to find in a scruffy anarchist newspaper John Kelly's description of a speech to the United Nations by Dr. Patrick Hillery as having been written by "some first class Iveagh House official . . . whom we can expect to emerge from anonymity into the public view according as the incompetence of his political superiors becomes more and more unbearable."

The quality of sheer contempt for much of what passes for public utterance is, in Kelly's vision of the machinery of State, quite extraordinary; "I believe one of the worst jobs is that of somebody in the public service who has to write a Minister's speech. For all I know, he comes in in the morning with the same kind of bothers at home we all have, with screaming children and so on, and he groans to himself 'What will I put in this man's mouth? I had better fire in something about the cost of oil.' He gets a few words down. I always find that is a help. 'There is a growing realisation' is always a great start to a sentence."

That this contempt is rooted in a Home Ruler's view of Irish History, a view forward, as it were, from the great days of our Victorian parliamentarians, looking at the mess the Christian Brothers upstarts have made of this country can be judged from John Kelly's reaction to a speech by Charles Haughey on the need to get away from "Victorian economics."

"What would Mr. Gladstone have said about a State which annually runs a colossal deficit on current account? . . What would Mr. Disraeli have thought of a country like this with £20billion of a national debt?. . . Is there any chance that the dear queen might have authorised such a thing, or any of her ministers from first to last — Lord Melbourne, Lord Palmerston, Lord Salisbury?"

It is from this same perspective that John Kelly's much-vaunted calls for Fianna Fáil and Fine Gael to settle their piffling differences was possible. Like everything else about the State, the trauma of its first years is a bit of a joke; "I sometimes regret that so much of the bitterness has gone out of public life here."

From the point of view of the usurped ruling-class-in-waiting, the Civil War split is comparable to an over enthuastic sporting rivalry and "has still not developed an ideological or other base than personal rivalry sustained by a group ethos no more profound than that which sustains football teams."

This set of undercurrents melts in Kelly's case into traditional right-wing Cold War thinking. The State is so fragile that we may all "wake up one morning" and find that we are being run by the Cubans and the East Germans. And the State is so contemptible that the best thing it can do is to shrink away to the primitive machinery from which it began — "the original elementary functions which alone justify its existence — and loosen the grip of the "farrow of cannibal piglets" (the young, the unemployed, the sick?) which is sucking it dry.

This similarity to right-wing mania everywhere, though, shouldn't blind us to the particular Irish roots of the native version.

What's important about that particularity is the notion of an establishment as an alienated minority which it carries with it. Since our other establishment — the country-and-western alliance — also manages (even though it has run the country for most of the last 70 years) to think of itself as made up of outsiders, persecuted by shmart Dublin 4 types and their meeja sidekicks, we end up with two sets of people who have immense power but yet manage, through their complementary myths of persecution and marginalisation, to avoid responsibility for the state of the place.

Both groups, even when they are in power, manage to talk as if they were the opposition, waffling on about how things are shocking entirely and somebody should do something about them. The myth of Dublin 4 is one way of ensuring that the buck stops nowhere.

RISKS?

"The people who choose to play may start the evening with equal piles of chips, but as the play progresses, those piles will become unequal. By the end of the evening some will be big winners, others big losers. In the name of the ideal of equality, should the winners be required to repay the losers! That would take all the fun out of the game."—
Milton Friedman

If there's no such thing as original sin, neither is there such a thing as original excuse. As the sincere and genuine outrage manifested even in the act of resignation by the protagonists of some of the recent affairs has shown, nobody ever really believes they have done wrong. There is always a justification: I didn't do it and if I did do it I didn't know I was doing it and if I did know about it, it was for my kids and anyway where would society be if it didn't have people like me. In the absence of justice, there is always justification.

We always have moralities that justify ourselves to ourselves. And the most powerful morality at work in this society, as in other western societies in the last decade, has been the morality of competition. Life is a free competition and whoever wins is as much entitled to the gold medal as the winner of an Olympic race. The losers will whinge and gripe, but only because they are losers. Instead of whinging, they should do something for themselves and start to compete.

I thought it would be worthwhile, therefore to play a little game of snakes and ladders this morning. The board is Irish society. The dice are the chances that any of the players have at any particular moment. Our two players are Michael, whose father is a businessman, and Mick, whose father is unemployed or sometimes in low-paid work. Neither Michael nor Mick is yet born, each is a miraculous amalgam of codes and cells, an embryonic human being.

For the purposes of the game we will assume that each of them has encoded in his cells the same amount of genetically-determined ability. They're both turning there in the aqueous space of the womb, both listening to the same heartbeat tattoo. On the throw of the dice, which will not be pure chance but determined by the actual way Irish society works (I have taken many of the figures from Robbie Gilligan's excellent new book *Irish Child Care Services*) will depend their advancement up the board.

The first throw is to get into the game, to be born. Even there in the womb, Michael gets the kinder throw of the dice. Michael is much less likely than Mick to have a mother who smokes, or takes drugs, or drinks too much during pregnancy. But even apart from these risks, Mick is much more likely to have a complicated birth, since his mother is more likely to have a previous obstetric history of caesarean section, toxaemia or bleeding.

Michael's mother, on the other hand, though she is less at risk, will have received much more medical attention before the birth and will receive more after it. Mick, in fact has a vastly better chance of not getting into the game at all. He has 22 chances in 1000 of dying in or around the birth. Michael has less than 2 chances in 1000.

Still, both probably do get onto the board but Michael, clever boy, is already well ahead.

The second throw is coming up and Michael scores a six on the dice, Mick scores a one. This is because the throw is about breast-feeding and Michael's mother is six times more likely to breast-feed him than Mick's is. This has advantages for Michael. He is less likely to get allergies and less likely to get dehydrated. Mick has a better chance of laying down extra fat cells which will make his weight more difficult to control in later life.

If you think this is just too mean to poor Mick, we'll give him another throw. This time he comes up trumps. His mother starts to breast-feed him. Six weeks later because of stress and lack of energy and the pressure of economic demands, she is twice as likely as Michael's mother to have given it up.

Nice one, Michael. As you suck away happily, the thought might occur to you that "risk taking" has worked out pretty well for you so far. So far, Mick has taken most of the risks, but you're the one who's going to be an entrepreneur.

After these ladders for Michael and snakes for Mick, both have moved off a milk diet and onto solid foods. On the third throw of the dice, Mick will let out a little yelp of delight. Between the ages of one and four, he's three times more likely to be bought sweets every day. Unfortunately he's hit a big snake pretty quickly.

His diet is worse than Michael's, his teeth get more cavities, he is twice as likely to miss breakfast when he goes to school, he doesn't get to the dentist as often, and when he does go he's more likely to have a bad tooth extracted rather than filled.

Already, his height and weight are considerably inferior to Michael's.

The fourth throw of the dice is on the mind not on the body. Mick and Michael's ultimate adjustment to their lives will depend hugely on the mental well-being of their parents. Again, Mick throws a one and Michael throws a six, since it is six times more likely that Mick's parents will enter a psychiatric hospital than that Michael's will.

In the case of schizophrenia where having a parent with the illness makes you much more likely eventually to develop it yourself, Mick is 21 times more likely to be at risk in this way than Michael. And even short of these dramatic problems, Mick's parents are very much more likely to suffer from stress and depression, with all that

219

that means for the relationship between a parent and a child, than Michael's are.

Even before Mick and Michael are 11 years old, Mick is twice as likely as Michael to be regarded as maladjusted at school. Already, Mick has a much greater chance of having been labelled a loser.

Staying with the mind for the fifth throw, Mick will surely be able to find comfort in the world of books, to enter new experiences and learn from them. Maybe his imagination will be fuelled by all the sliding down snakes he's already had to endure, while Michael's progress in the game has been too undifferentiated in it's success.

Even at primary school though, Mick has already a one-in-two chance of having a reading age that is 18 months behind his actual age. He has at least three times the chances of having severe reading difficulties than Michael has.

We now come to the last throw of the dice. Mick and Michael are both 15. Mick now has a one-in-three chance of leaving school with no qualification at all. This in turn will have a huge impact on all subsequent throws of the dice, because this will determine both what sort of jobs Mick and Michael might get, and what their chances of being unemployed might be.

Even if Michael leaves school after the Leaving Cert, he still has twice the chance of getting a job as Mick has with his Junior Cert. Michael has a 19 times better chance of getting into third-level education than Mick has. On the other hand Mick has a fifteen times better chance of landing the jackpot of unemployment. He also has six times Michael's chances of falling foul to the law before he's 20.

Not much of a competition is it? Not much of an advertisement for the joys of risk taking, either. Mick runs all the risks and hits all the snakes. Michael scoots up all the ladders. By now, they have both got bored with the predictability of the game. Mick has taken up Scrabble and Michael is playing Monopoly.

As Michael buys up properties and builds his houses and hotels and raids the Community Chest, he is muttering to himself about the ingratitude of those who don't know what it's like to take chances. If he gets caught building a hotel he shouldn't have built, he'll explain he was just trying to give his kids an extra start in life, a leg up in the game.

It is, after all, a tough, competitive world out there.

Acknowledgements

These pieces, which together try to describe what it feels like to be Irish in the 1990s, are a mixture of journalism and essays. Almost all of them start from news items, radio interviews, political speeches - the flotsam and jetsam of the public world. If they make use of history, of art, and of theatre, they use them only as surfboards on which to try to stay upright while the waves of events rush forward. I make no claim to detachment from the immediacy of things as they happen. The aim of bringing them together, indeed, is to suggest some of the lineaments of the Irish culture that is replacing the one invented a hundred years and now all but disappeared.

Many of these pieces, indeed, were written for *The Irish Times* as responses to immediate political circumstances — elections, scandals, referenda. I have left them as they were published first, since whatever value they have is inextricable from the times and the events to which they respond. I am very grateful to *The Irish Times*, to its editor Conor Brady and to op-ed page editors Dick Grogan and Joe Breen both for publishing them in the first place and for giving me permission to re-publish them here.

Other pieces, though, are published here for the first time, and are perhaps more leisurely in their approach. Nevertheless, these too were conceived in order to meet deadlines, and in response to particular occasions and provocations. *The Lie of the Land* was developed in part for the Oriel Gallery in Swansea, in part for the New Tate Gallery in Liverpool, and in yet another part for the Glenstal Ecumenical Conference in 1993. An earlier version of *Going Native* was written for the SOFEIR conference in Lyon in 1993. *Tourists in Our Own Land* began life as a lecture for the Yeats International Summer School in Sligo in 1993. Many of these ideas, in turn, grew out of the BBC Radio 4 series, *Notes from Laputa,* produced by Mary Price, which I wrote in 1993. *Kick the Can* was first published as part of the book *Invisible Cities*, published by Raven Arts Press, and resulted from a good kicking from Dermot Bolger, as, indeed, does this book.